KEY FACTS KEY CASES

EU Law

KEY FACTS KEY CASES

The Key Facts Key Cases revision series is designed to give you a clear understanding and concise overview of the fundamental principles of your law course. The books' chapters reflect the most commonly taught topics, breaking the law down into bite-size sections with descriptive headings. Diagrams, tables and bullet points are used throughout to make the law easy to understand and memorise, and comprehensive case checklists are provided that show the principles and application of case law for your subject.

Titles in the series:

Contract Law

Criminal Law

English Legal System

Equity & Trusts

EU Law

Family Law

Human Rights

Land Law

Tort Law

For a full listing of the Routledge Revision range of titles, visit www.routledge.com/law

KEY FACTS KEY CASES

EU Law

Chris Turner

Routledge
Taylor & Francis Group

LONDON AND NEW YORK

First published 2014
by Routledge
2 Park Square, Milton Park, Abingdon, Oxon OX14 4RN

and by Routledge
711 Third Avenue, New York, NY 10017

Routledge is an imprint of the Taylor & Francis Group, an informa business

© 2014 Chris Turner

British Library Cataloguing in Publication Data
A catalogue record for this book is available from the British Library

Library of Congress Cataloging in Publication Data
A catalog record for this book has been requested

ISBN: 978–0–415–83328–8 (pbk)
ISBN: 978–1–315–88042–6 (ebk)

Typeset in Helvetica
by RefineCatch Limited, Bungay, Suffolk

Contents

Preface

The Key Facts Key Cases series is a practical and complete revision aid that can be used by students of law courses at all levels from A Level to degree and beyond, and in professional and vocational courses also.

The Key Facts Key Cases series is designed to give a clear view of each subject. This will be useful to students when tackling new topics and is invaluable as a revision aid.

Most chapters open with an outline in diagram form of the points covered in that chapter. The points are then developed in a structured list form to make learning easier. Supporting cases are given throughout by name and for some complex areas facts are given to reinforce the point being made.

The Key Facts Key Cases series aims to accommodate the syllabus content of most qualifications in a subject area, using many visual learning aids.

Each title in the Key Facts Key Cases series now incorporates a Key Cases section at the end of each chapter which is designed to give a clear understanding of important cases. This is useful when studying a new topic and invaluable as a revision aid. Each case is broken down into fact and law. In addition many cases are extended by the use of important extracts from the judgment or by comment or by highlighting problems. Cases marked in bold in the key facts section signify that they have then been included with further detail in the key cases checklist at the end of the chapter.

In some instances students are reminded that there is a link to other cases or material. If the link case is in another part of the book, the reference will be clearly shown. Links will be to additional cases or materials that do not feature in the book.

To give a clear layout, symbols have been used at the start of each component of the case. The symbols are:

 Key Facts – These are the basic facts of the case.

 Key Law – This is the major principle of law in the case.

Key Judgment – This is an actual extract from a judgment made on the case.

 Key Comment – Influential or appropriate comments made on the case.

 Key Problem – Apparent inconsistencies or difficulties in the law.

 Key Link – This indicates other cases which should be considered with this case.

The Key Link symbol alerts readers to links within the book and also to cases and other material especially statutory provisions which are not included.

The law is as I believe it to be on 1 April 2013.

Table of Cases

1

The constitution and character of EU law

▶ 1.1 Origins and background

1.1.1 The concept of a single Europe

1. The UK tends towards 'euro-scepticism', so two misconceptions usually prevail:
   - that the idea of a united Europe is new;
   - that the EU legal order is a haphazard process of co-operation between Member States.

2. The Roman Empire is one possible starting point, with several subsequent attempts at European unity or aspirations towards it:
   - Papal view of 'Christendom';
   - Charlemagne's 'Holy Roman Empire';
   - Henry IV of France and the 'Christian Commonwealth of Europe';
   - Even the aspirations of Napoleon and Hitler;
   - European unity has also been a common theme of every major political philosopher, e.g. Kant, Rousseau, Nietzsche, Marx.

3. So history possibly favours the 'europhiles', with 'euro-scepticism' a more recent nationalist hostility to the EU.

4. Ironically, a federal Europe originated as a British idea.

5. The intellectual architect of 'Europe' was Jean Monnet.

1.1.2 The background to the European Union (Community)

1   There were various attempts at integration in the 19th and 20th centuries.

2   These were based on need to avoid war, particularly after the Second World War.

3   There were two key factors:

    ● the Treaty of Versailles failed and led to the rise of Nazism;

    ● so it was vital to bring Germany within the European 'partnership'.

4   Churchill, in his 1947 Zurich speech, said 'We must build a kind of United States of Europe'.

5   The European Union of Federalists was established in 1947.

6   Continental advocates of union argued for 'supranational bodies' in the Montreux Resolution 1947.

7   Various intergovernmental agreements created new world or European organisations at this time: IMF; GATT; OEEC; The Council of Europe; Benelux Union.

1.1.3 The creation of the Treaties

1   The Treaties originated in the 'Schumann Plan' following principles established in the 'Marshall Plan' in the USA:

    ● the narrow aspect was placing French and German coal and steel production under a 'higher authority';

    ● the wider agenda was to move towards a federal Europe.

2   The plan led to the first Treaty: European Coal and Steel Community Treaty (ECSC Treaty) – Treaty of Paris 1951.

    ● It also devised an institutional framework of communities (later to be added to by the European Court of Justice).

    ● Monnet was made first President of ECSC.

3   This was followed by an unsuccessful initiative to create a European Defence Community.

4   Further integration and a move towards the establishment of supranational institutions came with the two Treaties of Rome 1957 – the European Atomic Energy Community Treaty (EURATOM) and the European Economic Community Treaty (EC Treaty).

5   The latter resulted from the Spaak Committee Report and a recommendation for the creation of a 'common market'.

6   The Treaties were originally signed by only six countries: France, Italy, Germany, Belgium, the Netherlands and Luxembourg.

- Different countries had different things to gain.

- This meant that integration was always dogged by national self-interest.

- This ensured that development would be 'incremental' and that principle would be sacrificed to pragmatism.

- As a result, the UK stayed out.

7   Objectives of the Treaties were to be achieved by two means:

- the creation of a common (now single) market and common policies;

- monetary union.

8   The former has always predominated and dictated the character of the EU (formerly the Community).

9   So, the establishment of the 'four freedoms', the removal of internal barriers and, more importantly, the new legal order were required.

▶ 1.2 The development of the Treaties (from EC, ECSC, EURATOM, to SEA, TEU, ToA, ToN and ToL)

1   The original Treaties have been supplemented and modified, firstly within the Community and then in an evolving Union.

2   The early years of the Community, from 1958 to 1965, were characterised by economic boom:

- good progress was made towards the creation of a 'customs union', i.e. dismantling of tariffs;

- but there was far less progress towards an actual common market;

- some competition policy was put in place;

- some moves were made towards free movement of workers;

- but there was over-prominence of the Common Agricultural Policy (CAP);

- good work was done by the European Court of Justice (ECJ) in defining the character of the legal order.

3   The Common Market should have been achieved within the 'transitional period', i.e. 12 years from 1957, in three four-year periods.

4   However, in 1965–66 de Gaulle created a crisis over qualified majority voting, with France withdrawing from participation in the Council.

5   This was partly resolved by the Luxembourg Accords, which effectively created a sort of veto for Member States on major issues (of uncertain future with commitment to integration in the Treaty on European Union).

6   In many ways the years from then until 1986 and the adoption of the Single European Act (SEA) are seen as years of stagnation in terms of integration.

- This can partly be explained by economic recession and the retreat into national interest (particularly the UK).
- However, in other areas the community did develop:
  - i) by enlargement (firstly to 12, then to 15 countries);
  - ii) by broadening (developing policy in and outside the original Treaty objectives – although some took some time to be fully adopted because of national self-interest, e.g. Social Charter);
  - iii) judicial activism of the ECJ (in defining supremacy and developing direct effect and its alternatives).

7   The effective 're-launch' of the Community came in 1986.

8   There were three principal reasons for this:

- the Commission presidency of Jacques Delors;
- a commitment to further integration by key political figures in the Member States (notably Chancellor Kohl in Germany and President Mitterand in France);
- the growing realisation that survival depended on an effective EC;
- the adoption of the Single European Act (with a set time scale of 1992 for implementation of the Single Market).

9   SEA 1986 included five major provisions:

- a definition of the internal market and the 1992 deadline;
- a new law-making process in co-operation with Parliament on certain measures;
- creation of the Court of First Instance to support the ECJ;
- provision for compulsory rather than *ad hoc* meetings of a European Council twice yearly (formally recognised);
- the idea of European Political Co-operation.

10 Treaty on European Union (TEU) (signed at Maastricht) followed in 1992.

   ● It did not include everything most states wanted.

   ● The UK was allowed to opt out of the most important parts in order to secure a treaty at all.

   ● So the desired environmental laws were not included.

   ● There was only agreement to co-operate on defence and justice, rather than being part of the legal order.

   ● Eleven of the then 12 agreed on the Social Chapter, but the UK opted out, thus necessitating the protocol procedure.

   ● But it did create the union and the idea of European citizenship – though not within the legal order.

11 The Treaty of Amsterdam (ToA) 1997 then re-numbered the Articles of the EC Treaty, and the UK signed the Social Chapter.

12 The Treaty of Nice (ToN) introduced major changes to the composition of the institutions, voting procedures, enlargement and 'enhanced co-operation'.

13 A draft constitution to put all aspects of the EU within the legal order was accepted as the EU Constitution. Some states ratified it by parliamentary vote but it was rejected in referenda in France and the Netherlands, leaving some doubt as to how the EU would develop. A 'two-track Europe' was one possibility.

14 The Lisbon Treaty (ToL) introduced similar modifications to the Treaties, but without the single constitutional document. The Treaty is now in force.

▶ 1.3 Basic aims and objectives of EU law and supranationalism

1 The objectives of the EU are quite simply stated originally in the EC Treaty and now in the TFEU: 'to promote throughout the [EU] a harmonious development of economic activities, a continuous, balanced expansion, an increase in stability, an accelerated raising of the standard of living and quality of life and closer relations between the states belonging to it and sustainable development of economic activities, a high level of employment and of social protection, equality between men and women, sustainable and non-inflationary growth, a high degree of competitiveness and convergence of economic performance, a high

level of protection and of improvement of the quality of the environment, and economic and social cohesion among the Member States.'

2   It is easy to assume that the constitution of the EU is no more than what
    is laid down in the Treaties, but this would be only partly true because
    all constitutions are defined by how they are interpreted in the Courts.

3   The EU constitution has the added complication of being founded in
    Treaty relationships entered into by sovereign states (one reason why
    the EU tried to create a written EU Constitution).

4   So, the first problem is identifying how Treaties come to be incorporated
    in Member States' law. There are two approaches:

    ● Monist constitutions – these include France and the Netherlands.
      The Treaty is automatically incorporated into the national legal
      system at the point of ratification.

    ● Dualist constitutions – these include Germany, Italy, Belgium and,
      of course, the UK where the Treaty is only incorporated after enact-
      ment. (In the UK this was by the European Communities Act 1972.)

5   The result can be a wide variance in how the Treaties are interpreted
    and applied.

6   For the legal order of the EU to function, the institutions must be 'supra-
    national', i.e. in relation to those things covered by the Treaties, they
    take precedence over national institutions.

7   The ECJ, in administering and defining EU law, and the principle of
    'supranationalism' has become vital to the role of ensuring the universal
    application of the Treaties:

    ● 'To avoid disparities arising out of different national approaches to
      the incorporation of [EU] law and to ensure uniformity in its applica-
      tion, the Court of Justice has developed its own jurisprudence on the
      Supremacy of EC (now EU) law.' (Penelope Kent: *The Law of the
      European Union*, Longman)

    ● 'ECJ has uniformly and consistently been the most effective integra-
      tion institution in the EU. Its role was established in Art 164 (now
      repealed): "The Court shall ensure that in the interpretation and
      application of this Treaty the law is observed." From its very incep-
      tion in the Treaty, the ECJ set about establishing its hierarchical
      authority as the ultimate court of constitutional review. In this area
      two areas in particular are important. First there is the role of the
      ECJ in controlling member state courts, and, second, there is the role
      of the Court in managing the incessant inter-institutional struggles.'
      (Ian Ward: *A Critical Introduction to European Law*, Butterworths)

8   In respect of the former of these two – defining the relationship between the Community legal order and the Member States – three crucial factors apply:

- the doctrine of Supremacy (or Primacy) of EU law;

- the Art 267 reference procedure;

- the doctrine of direct effect as well as indirect effect and state liability developed by the ECJ to ensure that citizens can enforce their rights.

▶ 1.4 The European Union

1.4.1 General

1   The European Union finally came into force in 1993, only after ratification of the TEU by Member States.

2   The TEU created an entirely new structure, over and above that of the EC.

3   Between the ToN and ToL, the constitution was described as the 'three pillars':

- Pillar 1: comprised the legal order of the original Treaties, added to by economic and monetary union – so the other pillars are outside the scope of the legal order.

- Pillar 2: co-operation towards common foreign and security policy.

- Pillar 3: Police and judicial co-operation in criminal matters (originally co-operation towards common systems on justice and home affairs).

4   Pillars 2 and 3 were found in Titles V and VI and were not specifically incorporated into UK law.

5   There was debate over whether it was accurate to speak of EU law rather than EC law. Since the two extra pillars created by the TEU had no foundation in law but were based on co-operation, and since the law stemmed from the EC Treaty not the TEU, it was probably most accurate to use EC to refer to law, and EU to refer to the geographical unit formed by the 27 states.

6   Following the Treaty of Lisbon, all three pillars are incorporated into the Union with the same force and there is now e.g. a High Representative of the Union for Foreign Affairs and Security Policy.

1.4.2 The institutions of the Union

1   Before the Treaty of Lisbon there were strictly speaking no EU institutions; these were EC institutions. Now they are all institutions of the EU.

2   Article 3 (now repealed) of TEU provides that 'The Union shall be served by a single institutional framework . . .'.

3   Following the Treaty of Lisbon, the institutions are now the institutions of the EU with mostly the powers and duties proscribed for them under the original EC treaty.

1.4.3 The objectives of the Union

1   The objectives of the original Treaties were modified and amended over time by SEA and then TEU.

2   The objectives of the EU after ToL are:

- free movement of citizens;
- establishment of the internal market;
- balanced economic growth;
- a competitive social market economy;
- full employment, social progress;
- protection of the environment;
- promotion of scientific and technological advance;
- combating social exclusion and discrimination;
- promotion of social justice;
- equality between men and women;
- protection of the rights of children;
- promotion of economic, social and territorial cohesion;
- respect for cultural and linguistic diversity;
- economic and monetary union.

1.4.4 Common foreign and security policies

1   Between the TEU and ToL, this was Pillar 2 of the EU based on co-operation between Member States rather than having the legal force of the Community.

2   Now the ToL has merged the three pillars although special procedures exist.

3   There is also now a High Representative of the Union for Foreign Affairs and Security Policy – the role of which includes:

- conducting common foreign and security policy (Art 18(2) TEU);
- chairing the Foreign Affairs Council (Art 18(3) TEU);
- acting as a Vice-President of the Commission (Art 18(4) TEU).

4   By Art 24(2) TEU the EU is to pursue common policies and work for a high degree of co-operation in international relations – and by Art 26(1) TEU the European Council sets out the strategic interests.

5   Common foreign and security policy now includes:

- a solidarity clause in the event of terrorism;
- that international agreements can be made with one or more states or international organisations.

6   Art 42 TEU provides for a common security and defence policy including sharing military assets.

1.4.5 Area of freedom, security and justice

1   This was first introduced in TEU as the third pillar as 'Justice and Home Affairs' and was later changed in ToA to 'Police and judicial co-operation in criminal matters'.

2   Now it is referred to in Art 20 TEU and in Arts 67–89 TFEU.

3   It includes such areas as immigration and asylum seeking – Art 80 TFEU, and judicial co-operation in criminal matters – Art 83(1) TFEU.

4   Art 67(1) TFEU recognises respect for the 'fundamental rights and different legal systems and traditions of Member States'.

5   Legislation is now by the Ordinary Legislative Procedure (formerly the co-decision procedure) and is by qualified majority voting.

1.4.6 Final provisions of the TEU

1   The EC Treaty provided simple mechanisms for amending certain issues.

2   Now, other amendments must be made through TEU procedure:

- the Commission or Member State submits an amendment to the Council;

- the Council decides to hold an intergovernmental conference after consulting with the Commission and Parliament;
- a unanimous vote in the conference results in the amendment being sent to Member States for ratification.

3   Accession is to the Union:

- Croatia became a Member State on 1 July 2013;
- there are five countries with candidate status: Iceland, Montenegro, the Former Yugoslav Republic of Macedonia, Serbia and Turkey;
- there are also a number of other potential applicants: Albania, Bosnia and Herzegovina and Kosovo;
- applications require unanimous approval of Council and assent of Parliament;
- applicants fulfilling the necessary criteria have been eligible for entry since 2002 – Turkey's application has been unsuccessful so far because of its human rights record.

4   The EC Treaty made no mention of secession. Now Art 50 TEU states that 'Any member state may decide to withdraw from the Union in accordance with its own constitutional requirements'.

1.4.7 Some criticisms of the TEU

1   The UK reduced the scope of the Treaty by opting out of almost all the positive parts.

2   This led to fragmentation and the creation of various protocols, described by some commentators as having no basis in the legal order.

3   So Maastricht was a surrender to national interests, e.g. subsidiarity, but this seems contradictory as union is a concept that implies a federal system.

4   The 'democratic deficit' was increased, not decreased:

- the Commission was still powerful, and still undemocratic;
- Parliament was increasingly democratic, but still relatively ineffective;
- the Council was still the major power;
- so supranationalism was once again sacrificed for national interests.

5   However, subsequent Treaties, including ToA, ToN and ToL, have introduced significant institutional reform.

2 The Institutions of the European Union

The Council

- Fluid membership depending on subject discussed.
- The real law maker.
- Law is passed by qualified majority voting or unanimous voting, e.g. in developing Treaties.

Commission

- 'Civil service' with 24,000 staff.
- 27 Commissioners at present, each with Directorates General.
- Has three principal roles: drafting legislation; 'watchdog' of the Treaties; executive functions, e.g. implementing policy.

THE INSTITUTIONS

Parliament

- Democratically elected – numbers of MEPs based on importance of state.
- Consultative and amending role in legislation.
- Can censure Commission and affect non-compulsory budget.

Other institutions

- The General Court – helps ease ECJ workload.
- COREPER helps prepare Ministers for Council work.
- Committee of Regions and Economic and Social Committee – consultation.
- Court of Auditors – reviews expenditure.
- European Council – twice-yearly summit.

European Court of Justice

- 27 *Judges Rapporteurs* plus Advocates-General:
- hear Art 267 referrals from Member States; and
- Art 258 infringement actions against Member States; and
- Art 263 (abuse of powers), Art 265 (failure to act), Art 340 (action for damages) all against EU institutions.

▶ 2.1 The development of the Institutions

1   Concept and character of the Institutions begins with the ECSC.

2   This required supranational bodies working independently of the Member States.

3   The ECSC introduced the idea of 'community', with the following main features:

- distinct legal personality;

- represented by autonomous institutions;

- Member States ceded some national sovereignty to Institutions for defined purposes.

4   The first Institution was the 'High Authority', with power to make legally binding decisions.

- Supplemented by a 'Common Assembly' – representative of Member States.

- Added to by a 'Special Council of Ministers' – with some legislative powers.

- Completed initially by a 'Court of Justice' to 'ensure that the law was observed'.

5   EEC and EURATOM Treaties followed the same pattern.

- Establishing 'communities' with four key Institutions.

- High Authority was replaced by a Commission with more limited powers.

6   A convention at the same time created a single Assembly and a single Court of Justice to represent all three communities.

7   The Brussels Treaty 1967 (Merger Treaty) established a single Council, and High Authority and two Commissions merged into one Commission – but communities kept separate identities.

8   The EU has a unique institutional structure:

- it is not like any international organisation;

- nor like a parliamentary democracy;

- it has no clear separation of powers, but does have separation of interests;

- it has a complex legislative process and an executive without real executive powers;

- its institutions all have broad autonomy and their own rules of procedure;

- but the overriding ruler of the EU is the Treaties – everything must conform with their objectives;
- and the Court of Justice exercises supervisory jurisdiction.

9   The Institutions have been added to over the years:

- Art 4 EC Treaty led to an Economic and Social Committee and a Court of Auditors – made independent by TEU;
- Art 4 also allowed COREPER – Committee of Permanent Representatives;
- SEA established the Court of First Instance (now the General Court);
- TEU created a Committee of the Regions;
- TEU also provided for a European Investment Bank and European Central Bank.

10 The role of the Institutions has also gradually changed:

- new Institutions have added complexity but not necessarily improvement;
- the balance of power between Council and Commission has shifted;
- Council's powers have increased;
- Parliament's role has increased.

▶ 2.2 The Council

1   This was formerly referred to as the Council of Ministers – after TEU it was the Council of the European Union; after ToL it is now the Council.

2   The Council is a fluid concept with floating membership:

- 'Council consists of authorised representatives of each state';
- the identity of the Minister depends on the subject of discussion;
- but the original intention was a college of delegates.

3   ToL creates the concept of Team Presidencies for different configurations of Council other than foreign affairs.

4   The Council is the major legislative organ, although there are some exceptions. It consults Parliament and Economic and Social Committees, but makes the final decision on any legislation.

5   The voting procedure is of two main types:

- unanimous – required for certain prescribed areas and, since Luxembourg Accords, if vital national interests at stake;

- qualified majority – with minimum of 255 votes (representing 62% of the EU population) carrying a measure, so designed to prevent large states abusing small ones, but originally designed to be used *per se*.

6   The qualified majority system is based on differential weighting according to the size and influence of the state:

Germany, France, Italy, UK	29 votes each
Spain, Poland	27 votes each
Romania	14 votes
Netherlands	13 votes
Belgium, Czech Republic, Greece, Hungary, Portugal	12 votes each
Austria, Bulgaria, Sweden	10 votes each
Denmark, Ireland, Lithuania, Slovakia, Finland, Croatia	7 votes each
Cyprus, Estonia, Latvia, Luxembourg, Slovenia	4 votes each
Malta	3 votes

7   From 2014, the definition of the qualified majority will be a double majority so that, to be adopted, an act must have the support of at least 55% of the EU Member States and at least 65% of the population of the EU. A blocking minority must include at least four Member States. However, between November 2014 and March 2017, any Member State may request that the current weighted voting system be applied instead.

8   The Council has as its objective 'to ensure that the objectives set out in the Treaty are attained'.

9   But of course it is also a political body actually representing the interests of the individual Member States.

10 The Council is supplemented by two further processes:

- European Council: twice-yearly meetings of heads of state and Foreign Ministers – a political summit;
- COREPER: a permanent committee representing Member States – sifting through Commission proposals.

▶ 2.3 The European Commission

1   The Commission has the clearest claim to being a supranational body.

2   It is sometimes referred to as a civil service, but has much broader powers and roles.

3   It is currently composed of 27 Commissioners:

- by Art 245 currently one from each state;
- but from October 2014 it will be a number representing 2/3 of the number of Member States;
- chosen on grounds of general competence and 'whose independence is beyond doubt';
- they take an oath to be independent and not seek or take instructions from their Member State (Art 245);
- their Member State undertakes not to influence them;
- the appointment is for a five-year term;
- each Commissioner gets a Directorate General with specific responsibilities;
- the Commission also includes 24,000 staff.

4   The Commission is headed by a President, who holds office for a renewable two-year period.

5   The Commission is collegiate and acts by simple majority.

6   It has three principal responsibilities:

- it is the initiator of legislation under Art 352 and can draft proposals on anything covered by the Treaties;
- it is the watchdog of the Treaties – all Member States are obliged to achieve the objectives of the Treaties, and the Commission can deal with breaches of EU law by Member States through Art 258 proceedings;
- it has executive functions, for instance the Commission is responsible for implementing policy and also for the compulsory budget.

7   Through a process known as comity the Council can delegate power to the Commission, i.e. to produce detailed regulations following the passing of a framework regulation by the Council.

8   The Commission is sometimes also accountable to Parliament, e.g. Parliament can pass a motion of censure causing the Commission to resign (as occurred in 1999).

▶ 2.4 The European Parliament

1   This was originally known as the Assembly.

- It was not democratically elected.
- It comprised appointed nominees from Member State governments.
- It had no legislative power and was only consultative.

2   It has been an elected body since 1979.

- Elections are every five years.
- Total membership is now 754.

3   Membership depends on the size and importance of the particular Member State – 736 MEPs were elected in 2009 as follows:

Member State	Number of MEPs each
Germany	99
France, Italy, UK	72
Poland, Spain	50
Romania	33
Netherlands	25
Belgium, Greece, Portugal, Czech Republic, Hungary	22
Sweden	18
Austria	17
Bulgaria	17
Denmark, Finland, Slovakia	13
Ireland, Lithuania, Croatia	12
Latvia	8
Slovenia	7
Cyprus, Estonia, Luxembourg	6
Malta	5

4   These MEPs were elected before ToL, which increased the number to 754 until 2014, with provision for four additional for Spain, two each for

France, Sweden and Austria and one each for Italy, UK, Poland, Netherlands, Bulgaria, Latvia, Slovenia and Malta. After 2014 Germany will lose three.

5   MEPs sit by political groupings rather than by national interest, and there is no mandatory voting for Member State interests – MEPs are representatives, not delegates.

6   Voting is on a majority basis.

7   Parliament elects its own President and officials.

8   Parliament enjoys three main powers at present:

   ● it can censure the Commission (and such a censure in 1999 led to the resignation of the entire Commission);

   ● it has powers over the non-compulsory budget;

   ● it has a consultative role in legislation mostly through the co-decision procedure.

▶ 2.5 The Court of Justice

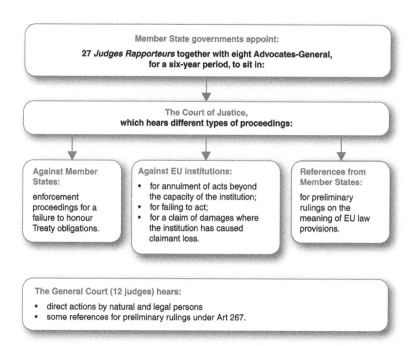

The work of the ECJ and General Court

1   This is not like any court in the English legal system.

2   It is composed of *Judges Rapporteurs* (the judges) and these are assisted by eight Advocates-General:

- one judge is appointed from each state (Art 19 TEU);
- by Art 253 TFEU they must be independent beyond doubt and judges or legal academics in their own country;
- they each serve a six-year term;
- but there is a staggered re-appointment system;
- removal of a judge is only possible if all colleagues agree that (s)he is unfit to serve;
- they appoint a president from their number;
- majority decision rules, with inquisitorial procedure and no dissenting judgments;
- cases used to involve a full court but after ToN can be a Grand Chamber of fewer judges;
- Advocates-General are appointed with the same requirements as for judges;
- cases are assigned to one of these first, who produces a reasoned opinion for the court – this does not have to be followed by the court but it may be.

3   The role of the court is:

- to ensure that in application and interpretation the law is observed;
- to provide a forum for resolving disputes between institutions, Member States, and individuals; and
- to protect individual rights.

4   The court hears five main types of action:

- Art 267 references from Member States for a preliminary ruling on an interpretation of EU law (known also as indirect actions);
- Art 258 actions against Member States for failing to implement Treaty obligations (a direct action known also as infringement proceedings);
- Art 263 actions against an institution for abuse of power;
- Art 265 actions against an institution for a failure to act;
- Art 340 actions for damages against an institution that has been responsible for loss to the individual, e.g. where the Commission has

failed to address a decision to a body engaging in anti-competitive practices and an individual suffers loss as a result.

5   It is important to note that the ECJ has been responsible for defining the Treaties and in particular has been instrumental in ensuring their enforcement through many landmark decisions, e.g. defining and developing the principles of supremacy, direct effect, indirect effect, state liability, etc.

6   Because of the excess workload of the ECJ and resultant delays, SEA also created a Court of First Instance (now the General Court):

● it has similar requirements to the ECJ and a judge from each Member State;

● its basic purpose is to ease the workload of the ECJ (but it has had limited success in doing so);

● it can hear staff cases; and direct actions under Arts 263 and 265 as well as for compensation arising from Art 340;

● also Art 267 references on a limited range of specific areas;

● there is a possible right of appeal to the ECJ.

▶ 2.6 The other major Institutions

1   Besides the four main Institutions of Council, Commission, Parliament and European Court of Justice, there are a number of other important Institutions – the first three have already been referred to.

2   The European Council:

● a twice-yearly summit of the heads of state and Foreign Ministers, focusing on political matters;

● in 1999 it gave a brief to the intergovernmental conference (IGC) to keep under review: the size and composition of the EU; weighting of votes in the Council of Ministers; extension to qualified majority voting.

3   COREPER – the Committee of Permanent Representatives:

● It is a permanent body of representatives from Member States, because of the fluid membership of the Council.

● It examines the Commission's legislative proposals for individual Ministers.

4   The General Court:

● set up initially in SEA;

● usually sits with three or five judges;

- jurisdiction was originally limited to staff cases, competition cases and anti-dumping cases but this has been extended;
- since 1993 it can hear all cases brought by natural or legal persons (including judicial review), but not those brought by the Institutions or by the Member States.

5   The Court of Auditors:
- This was created in 1975.
- It was designed to control and supervise the community budget.
- It was made a full Institution by TEU.
- It has qualified members from each state.
- It examines accounts of all revenue and expenditure.

6   The Economic and Social Committee (ESC):
- Membership is based on representation of social and economic activities, e.g. farmers, carriers, dealers, craftsmen, etc.
- It has a consultative role within the EU.
- It is consulted by either the Council or the Commission wherever they deem that it is appropriate to consult.
- It has a maximum of 350 members who are appointed by the Council.

7   The Committee of the Regions:
- This came into being in 1994 after TEU.
- Its membership comes from local and regional bodies, but not local or national government.
- It has a maximum of 350 members.
- It has a consultative role and is designed to bring regional influence to EU legislation.
- It usually gives opinions on things like education and training, culture, health, environmental issues and social cohesion.

8   The European Central Bank (ECB):
- In TEU provision was made in the Protocol to have a Central Bank to act for the EU.
- It is obviously a vital element of economic monetary union and the single currency.
- From January 1999 it has had responsibility for monetary policy in the EU.
- It is the only body allowed to issue euro banknotes.

3

The sources of European law

Primary Sources	**The Treaties:** ECSC; EURATOM; EC; SEA; TEU; ToA; ToN; ToL. Divides into: • Procedural Treaty Articles, e.g. Art 288 which identifies the legislation; or Art 258 an action against a Member State. • Substantive Treaty Articles, e.g. Art 157 Equal pay for men and women; or Art 45 the free movement of workers.

Secondary Sources

Legislation:

Regulations	Automatically law in Member States. They are generally applicable, binding in their entirety, and directly applicable.
Directives	Binding as to the effect to be achieved. Member States have an implementing period within which they must be incorporated in national law by whatever method.
Decisions	Addressed to a specific party, whether a company, individual, or Member State. They are then binding in their entirety on the party to whom they are addressed.
Recommendations	Have no legal force but are persuasive.
Opinions	Have no legal force but are persuasive.

Tertiary Sources

Case law of European Court of Justice

Vital because of:
- the power to ensure observance of Treaty objectives through Art 267 references;
- the judicial creativity of the ECJ in comparison to the relative inertia of the legislative bodies.

General Principles:
- proportionality, equality, legal certainty;
- protection of fundamental human rights;
- subsidiarity.

Acts adopted by representatives of Member State Governments meeting in Council.

National law of Member States.

Public International law.

The sources of EU Law

▶ 3.1 Primary sources – the Treaties

3.1.1 The structure of the Treaty on the Functioning of the European Union (replacing EC Treaty)

1   This begins with a preamble, which is useful for the ECJ for interpretation purposes.

2   It is then split into seven parts:
- principles – ground rules;
- citizenship – added by TEU and now in Art 20;
- policies of the Community – effectively the legal order;
- references to overseas relationships;
- external action by the Union;
- the institutions – empowerment and identification of roles etc.;
- general and final provisions, e.g. to enter into other treaties.

3   It also includes annexes, protocols and declarations.

4   The substantive law of the Treaty is also contained in numerous Articles.

3.1.2 The principles

1   Following ToL, Art 3 TEU has replaced Arts 2 and 3 EC Treaty and covers the basic principles and objectives of the EU.

2   The principles include:
- promoting peace and the well-being of the people;
- offering citizens an area of freedom, security and justice without internal frontiers;
- free movement of citizens recognising external border controls, immigration and asylum, and prevention of crime.

3   Objectives include:
- establishment of the internal market;
- balanced economic growth;
- a competitive social market economy;
- full employment, social progress;
- protection of the environment;

- promotion of scientific and technological advance;
- combating social exclusion and discrimination;
- promotion of social justice;
- equality between men and women;
- protection of the rights of children;
- promotion of economic, social and territorial cohesion;
- respect for cultural and linguistic diversity;
- economic and monetary union.

4   Art 3 TEU seeks to ensure that the EU acts within the limits of its powers and for the objectives assigned to it.

5   Art 4(3) TEU identifies the obligations of the Member States:

- 'to take all appropriate measures . . . to ensure fulfillment of the objectives arising out of the Treaty . . .';
- 'to abstain from any measure which could jeopardise the attainment of the objectives . . .'.

6   Art 18 TFEU identifies the basic principle of non-discrimination on the basis of nationality.

3.1.3 The Union policies

1   These are found in Part 3.

2   The most important are the 'Four Freedoms':

- free movement of goods (agriculture as a special category);
- free movement of persons;
- free movement of services (transport as a special category);
- free movement of capital.

3   Free movement of goods provides for the elimination of customs duties and quantitative restrictions between Member States to products originating in Member States, and products coming from non-Member States that are 'in free circulation':

- Art 30 governs the Customs Union – elimination of duties, etc.;
- Art 34 and Art 35 cover non-tariff barriers – elimination of quotas and bans.

4   Agriculture is subject to complex rules and a Common Agricultural Policy (CAP).

5   Free movement of persons and services are both guaranteed under the Treaties in Art 45, Art 49 and Art 56, and workers' families are also given protections in secondary legislation.

6   A common transport policy is also envisaged in the Treaty.

7   Free movement of capital is contained in TEU, all restrictions on movement of capital and payments are prohibited, and now policy is ultimately driven towards economic and monetary union.

8   Other main EU policies include:

● rules on anti-competitive practices in Art 101 and Art 102;

● tax provisions in Art 110;

● anti-discrimination in Art 157.

3.1.4 Rules on the institutions and on procedure

1   One of the most important procedural Articles is Art 288, which identifies and explains the different forms of legislation.

2   The relationship with Member States is partly defined in Art 267, which provides the mechanism for gaining interpretations of EU law from the ECJ.

3   The general rules regarding each of the institutions are in the TFEU:

● Parliament in Arts 223–234;

● Council in Arts 237–243;

● Commission in Arts 244–250;

● Court of Justice in Arts 251–281.

3.1.5 The general and final provisions

1   Provides the EU with a legal personality – so under Art 354 it can make arrangements with other international bodies.

2   The EU can be liable through its institutions (Art 340).

3   Powers are also given to Member States to derogate from Treaty obligations in certain extreme circumstances, e.g. security, serious internal disturbance or threat of external conflict, balance of payments crises.

4   The Council has very broad powers under Art 352 to legislate to do anything that is 'necessary to attain . . . an objective of the EU . . .'.

▶ 3.2 Secondary sources – Regulations, Directives and Decisions

3.2.1 The acts of the Institutions

1   Secondary legislation is a collective term used to describe all the various types of law the Institutions can make.

2   They are subordinate to primary law (the Treaties), and so cannot amend, repeal or alter the scope of a primary instrument.

3   So the Institutions may only act:

   ● in order to carry out their tasks;

   ● in strict accordance with the provisions of the Treaties;

   ● within the limits of the powers conferred upon them in the Treaties, specifically Art 288.

4   The TFEU at Art 288 provides that: 'In order to carry out their tasks and in accordance with the provisions of this Treaty, the European Parliament acting jointly with the Council [added by TEU], and the Commission shall make regulations and issue directives, take decisions, make recommendations or deliver opinions.'

5   The various forms of secondary legislation are described in Art 288 and it is their scope and effect that distinguishes them from each other.

3.2.2 Regulations

1   By Art 288: 'A regulation shall have general application. It shall be binding in its entirety and directly applicable in all Member States.'

   ● 'General application' means it applies to all Member States.

   ● 'Binding in its entirety' means Member States have no choice but to give effect to the regulation in its entirety.

   ● 'Directly applicable' means the regulation automatically becomes law in each Member State with no requirement for the state to do anything to implement it, and it may create rights and obligations directly enforceable in the national courts (*Bussone v Ministry of Agriculture* (1978)).

2   Regulations enter into force on the date specified in them.

3.2.3 Directives

1   By Art 288: 'A directive shall be binding, as to the result to be achieved, upon each Member State to which it is addressed, but shall leave to the national authorities the choice of form and methods.'

2   Directives are unlike regulations (which are uniform and directly applicable rules):

- they are used to ensure that Member States adapt their own laws for the application of common standards;
- they require Member States to choose the method of implementation within a set deadline;
- they are mainly used in areas where the diversity of national laws could have a harmful effect on the establishment or functioning of the Single Market.

3   So, whereas a regulation is applicable to Member States and individual citizens alike, a directive:

- is primarily intended to create legal obligations on the Member State;
- so is not intended to create directly enforceable rights for individuals, but the ECJ ensures that it does.

4   However, there are now important exceptions to this last point:

- vertical direct effect, which may be relied upon by the individual in the case of unimplemented directives if the claim is against the state or an 'emanation of the state' (*van Duyn* and *Ratti* and, of course, *Marshall* and, for an indication of what amounts to an emanation of the state, see also UK cases such as *Foster v British Gas* and *Doughty v Rolls-Royce*);
- the duty of 'uniform interpretation', which the ECJ derived originally from Art 10 EC Treaty (and is now in Art 4(3) TEU). Where there is a divergence between national law and the directive, the national law must be interpreted so as to give effect to the directive even where it remains unimplemented (the *Von Colson* principle, as developed by *Marleasing*) – the so-called principle of 'indirect effect');
- the *Francovich* principle, that while there can be no horizontal direct effect based on a directive as between non-state parties, an individual who has suffered loss as a result of the Member State's failure to implement a directive may claim damages from the state (so-called 'state liability' – *Grad v Finanzamt Traustein* 9/70).

3.2.4 Decisions

1   By Art 288: 'A decision shall be binding in its entirety upon those to whom it is addressed.'

2   The first feature of a decision is that it is the least easy to define of the legislative acts – it could be a legally binding measure in a specific legal form, but it could also be a non-binding, informal act laying down guidelines.

3   Its most striking effect is that it is immediately and totally binding on the addressee, and as a result may create rights for third parties.

	General applicability	Direct applicability	Direct effect
Treaty articles	Yes – they apply throughout the EU	Once Treaty is incorporated there is no need for further enactment of Articles	Yes – if they conform to the *Van Gend* criteria
Regulations	Yes – they apply throughout the EU	Yes – they require no further implementation	Yes – if they conform to the *Van Gend* criteria
Directives	Yes – they will be addressed to all states	No – they are an order, so require implementation	Only vertically if unimplemented or incorrectly implemented
Decisions	No – they are addressed to a particular individual	They are an order that must be complied with by the addressee	They may confer rights on other individuals affected by them

The effects of primary and secondary law

▶ 3.3 The process of legislating

3.3.1 Introduction

1   The process of legislating has been modified significantly as the result of different Treaties – one of the most significant features of the early legislative process was the so-called 'democratic deficit'.

2   Prior to the Treaty of Lisbon, there were four types of legislative procedure:

- the proposal (or consultation) procedure;
- the co-operation procedure;
- the co-decision procedure;
- assent.

3 The proposal procedure was the original legislative procedure in existence before the SEA.

4 Following the SEA the co-operation procedure was introduced to provide a straightforward method, involving the European Parliament (two readings) and to be passed by qualified majority voting for internal market measures – in fact this was largely removed by the Treaty of Amsterdam, and only survived in respect of Economic Monetary Union (EMU).

5 TEU introduced the co-decision procedure, which was subsequently modified or simplified by ToA and, as the Ordinary Legislative Procedure, it is now the main method of legislating following ToL.

6 The assent procedure, which was similar to the co-decision procedure, was introduced first in SEA and extended by TEU.

3.3.2 The Ordinary Legislative Procedure (formerly the co-decision procedure)

1 The co-decision procedure was introduced by TEU and simplified by the Treaty of Amsterdam and its use was extended by the Treaty of Nice. Now following ToL, as the Ordinary Legislative Procedure it is the main method of legislating.

2 It has given more power to Parliament, i.e. after Parliament proposing amendments, the Council must consider them and if they reject them then the act is not adopted, but final adoption of the measure is still with the Council.

3 There is also the possibility of a 'Conciliation Committee' made up of equal representation from Council and Parliament if Council does not accept all amendments.

4 It replaced the co-operation procedure in relation to internal market measures, and applies also to, for example, environment, transport, consumer protection and culture.

5 Following ToL, Art 5(1) TEU requires a process of conferral to limit the competences of the EU to legislate in particular areas. Where the EU institutions are not granted competence in the Treaties then there may be shared competence with the Member States, or the

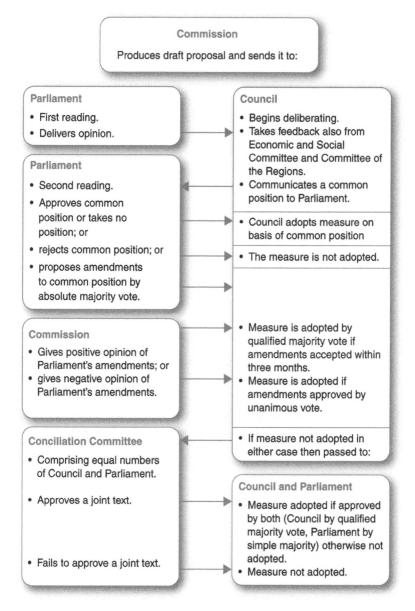

The Ordinary Legislative Procedure (formerly the co-decision procedure)

EU may act to support, co-ordinate or supplement the actions of Member States.

6   EU institutions have exclusive competence over: the customs union, competition rules, monetary policy for Member States in the Euro zone, marine biology and fisheries policy and international agreements.

3.3.3 The Special Legislative Procedure

1   Following ToL Art 289 TFEU provides for legislation by a Special Legislative Procedure.

2   This involves special cases where the Treaties provide for secondary legislation either:

- by Parliament with Council's involvement (must be adopted jointly); or

- by Council with Parliament's participation (Council only needs to consult Parliament).

3   Examples are under Art 64(3) TFEU and Art 86(1) TFEU.

▌ 3.4 Non-binding secondary legislation

1   Art 288 introduces the concept of 'soft laws', referring specifically to recommendations and opinions, but adds: 'Recommendations and opinions have no binding force.'

2   While having no legal force, they can be issued on any matter dealt with in the Treaties, and may be persuasive, particularly politically and morally: *Grimaldi* C-322/88.

3   Since TEU increasing use has been made of soft laws, particularly within the social context.

4   A classic example was the Commission Code of Practice on Sexual Harassment.

▌ 3.5 General principles of law

3.5.1 General

1   These are often unwritten principles (but not always, e.g. equality – Art 157, etc.).

2   These are generally developed by the ECJ, using as its authority the now repealed Art 220 EC – the general duty on the Court of Justice to ensure that EU law is observed.

3 They are nevertheless binding on the institutions, the Member States and individual citizens.

4 General principles are a familiar concept to those states with a 'civil' Roman law tradition.

5 So they are essentially a statement of values and basic standards that the court will use in interpretation.

6 They are broad enough to be generally acceptable as principle, but specific application can cause controversy.

7 Since much EU law is essentially administrative, some principles have derived from administrative law of France and Germany, but some has also derived from UK law.

3.5.2 Proportionality

1 This is now in TFEU Art 42: 'Any action by the EU shall not go beyond what is necessary to achieve the objectives of this treaty.'

2 The means used must be proportionate to the end to be achieved.

3 It derives from a German principle, *verhaltnismassigkeit*.

4 First stated in the *International Handelgessellschaft Case* 11/70: 'No burdens should be placed on the citizens except to the extent that it is necessary to achieve the purpose.'

5 So, if the burden is too great the court can disapply the measure (see *Bela Muhler Bergman v Grows Farm* 114/76 and *Watson (Lynne) and Alessandro Belmann* 118/75).

3.5.3 Equality

1 A general principle of equal treatment and non-discrimination.

2 Equal situations must always be treated equally unless there are objective justifications for doing otherwise.

3 By Art 18 TFEU: no discrimination on nationality.

4 Art 157 was originally a specific provision on gender discrimination on pay – now the Treaty includes the general aim of equality between men and women.

5 But the principle also obviously applies in internal organisation (*Sabbatini v Parliament* 20/71).

6 Equality now extended through various directives to include preventing discrimination on race, sexual orientation, disability, religion and belief, age, etc.

3.5.4 Legal certainty and procedural rights

1   The basic principle is that the law in its application must be predictable. So:

- there should be no retroactive laws (*Société pour l'exploitation des sucres v Commission* 88/76);
- there will be respect for acquired rights, which cannot later be withdrawn;
- a person is entitled to act according to legitimate expectations, i.e. as though the law still applies (*Commission v Council* 81/72);
- persons affected should be identifiable;
- language should be easily understood;
- a person is entitled to a fair hearing (*Transocean Marine Paint Association v The Commission* 17/74). Also found in some secondary legislation, e.g. Directive 64/221 derogations on free movement.

3.5.5 The protection of fundamental human rights

1   Now contained in Art 11 TFEU: 'shall respect fundamental rights guaranteed by the European Convention ... and from the constitutional traditions common to the Member States ...'.

2   A number of propositions emerge from this:

- *audi alteram partem* – fair hearings before imposition of a penalty (*Transocean Marine Paint*);
- penalty must be based on a clear, unambiguous case;
- no retroactive laws;
- no one should be subjected to two penalties;
- entitlement to legal assistance and representation;
- a person is protected from self-incrimination, so no requirement to answer leading questions;
- respect for private life and inviolability of premises (*X v Commission* 404/92).

3   It originates from the constitutions of certain Member States (*The International Handelgessellschaft Case* 11/70).

4   But the ECJ is prepared to recognise the significance of human rights (*Nold v The Commission* 4/73).

5   Although the EU is not a signatory to the European Convention on Human Rights it is possible to invoke Articles of the Convention (*R v Kirk* 63/83).

6   There is now also a Charter of Rights accepted at the Nice Summit.

3.5.6 Subsidiarity

1   There is some reference to subsidiarity in the founding Treaties – decisions should be taken as closely as possible to citizens affected by them.

2   It was incorporated in the Treaty as Art 5 by TEU at the UK's insistence: 'In areas which do not fall within its exclusive competence, the community shall take action, in accordance with the principle of subsidiarity, only if and in so far as the objectives of the proposed action cannot be sufficiently achieved by the Member States and can therefore, by reason of the scale or effects of the proposed action, be better achieved by the community.' Now in Art 4(1) TEU.

3   So there is a twofold test – EU action can only be justified if it serves an end which:

● cannot be achieved satisfactorily at national level; and

● can be achieved better at community level.

▶ 3.6 Case law of the ECJ

1   Unlike English law, continental 'civil' systems have no binding system of precedent, and the ECJ follows the same principles.

2   Any binding force in the judgment then rests on the principle of *res judicata*.

3   So, for future cases ECJ judgments act as moral rather than strictly legal authority, and in the strictest technical sense then the court's judgments are not a formal source of law.

4   However, there are a number of qualifying points:

● the court will not depart from its own rulings on law without pressing reasons, and judgments, if studied, show remarkable consistency;

● a ruling in a particular case has an inevitable impact beyond the case itself;

● the *Cilfit* rules on Art 267 references prevent repetitious references seeking new rulings on the same principle of law;

● the ECJ has proved over the years to be very proactive;

● indeed, many of the most definitive principles of EU law have originated in the ECJ, e.g. direct effect, indirect effect, state liability, etc.

Key Cases Checklist

3.5.2

Italy v Watson and Belmann 118/75 [1976] ECR 1185

Key Facts

A young English woman had settled in Italy with her Italian boyfriend but without obtaining the necessary work permit. When they split and the boyfriend reported her to Italian immigration authorities the penalty under Italian law was deportation.

Key Law

The ECJ held that, while the Italian State was clearly entitled to insist on procedures for entry within the scope of Directive 68/360 (now under Directive 2004/38) and to impose sanctions, its action was disproportionate to the required objective. The woman's Art 48 (now under Art 45 TFEU) rights had been infringed.

Key Link

R v Pieck 157/79 [1980] ECR 2171 p 59, which makes the same point on refusal of entry.

3.5.2

R v Intervention Board, ex p Man (Sugar) Ltd 181/84 [1985] ECR 2889

Key Facts

A sugar trader failed to apply for the necessary export licenses by the time specified. The bank where securities had to be lodged acted in accordance with Regulation 1880/83 and forfeited the securities, resulting in a loss of £1,670 to the trader. In the Art 234 reference (now under Art 267 TFEU) the trader's argument that the forfeiture procedure was disproportionate was accepted.

Key Law

The ECJ, in its preliminary ruling, identified that the licensing requirement under the Regulation was only for the purpose of ensuring sound management of the market. On this basis the total forfeiture provided for by the Regulation was disproportionate to the actual offence committed by the trader and was not valid according to the court.

Key Comment

The ECJ applies the principle both to national legislation introducing EU measures and to EU legislation, in either instance by determining whether the legislation goes beyond what is necessary to achieve the actual purpose in the Treaty.

3.5.3

P v S and Cornwall County Council C-13/94 [1996] All ER (EC) 397

Key Facts

A male employee of a college informed the Director of Studies that he was undergoing 'gender reassignment'. He began dressing as a woman and was then dismissed after undergoing some surgery. He brought an action for sex discrimination. In the reference the ECJ agreed.

Key Law

The ECJ took a broad view of sex discrimination and applied the principle of equality to the dismissal of a transsexual.

Key Problem

In *Grant v South West Trains Ltd* (1998) the court did not feel bound to apply the same principle of equality to same-sex couples. This was because the regulations applied equally whatever the relationship, man and man or woman and woman. However, this position is now changed under the Framework Directive.

Key Link

Prais v The Council 130/75 [1976] ECR 1589 p 128.

3.5.4

Mulder v Minister of Agriculture and Fisheries 120/86 [1988] ECR 2321

Key Facts

A dairy farmer entered into an agreement not to supply milk for five years in return for a payment. A regulation on milk quotas was then introduced while the agreement was still in force. The quota system contained no measures for farmers who were part of the agreement, as a result of which the farmer was prevented from supplying milk when his agreement ended. The reference to the ECJ confirmed that his rights were being infringed.

Key Law

The ECJ held that the farmer must be entitled to resume production and supply at the end of the agreement. He had a legitimate expectation based on the legal certainty of the agreement. He had legitimate expectations based on the agreement he had made in good faith.

3.5.4   *R v Ministry of Agriculture, Fisheries and Food, ex p Hamble (Offshore) Fisheries Ltd* [1995] 2 All ER 714

Key Facts

The Ministry introduced a stringent system for granting fishing licences so as to protect fish stocks in UK waters which had become overworked. The reference confirmed that the claimant's action could not succeed.

Key Law

The Court of First Instance (now the General Court) held that the principle of legitimate expectations could not apply and the rights of the holders of fishing licences were not infringed by the arrangements. This was because arrangements of this type must be allowed to cater for changes in circumstances and reduced fish stocks was a significant change in circumstances.

Key Judgment

'The principles of legal certainty and the protection of legitimate expectation are fundamental to European Community (now EU) law. Yet these principles are merely general maxims derived from the notion that the Community (now EU) is based on the rule of law and can be applied to individual cases only if expressed in enforceable rules . . . other principles . . . run counter to legal certainty and . . . the right balance will need to be struck.'

3.5.4

Union Nationale des Etraineurs et Cadres Techniques Professionels du Football (UNECTEF) v Heylens 222/86 [1987] ECR 4097

Key Facts

A Belgian football trainer possessed a Belgian diploma but was denied the right to take up training in France. He was not given any hearing nor was any reason given for the decision. The reference identified that his rights under Art 48 (now Art 45 TFEU) had been infringed.

Key Law

In the reference the ECJ held that this was a breach of process. Member States must provide both a proper hearing and a right to appeal.

Key Judgment

The court stated that: '[In] a question of securing the effective protection of a fundamental right conferred by the Treaty on Community (now EU) workers [they] must be able to defend that right under the best possible conditions and have the possibility of deciding, with a full knowledge of the relevant facts, whether there is any point in applying to the courts.'.

Key Link

Bosman v Royal Belgian Football Association and EUFA C-415/93 [1995] ECR I-4921 p 63.

3.5.5

J. Nold KG v Commission 4/73 [1974] ECR 491

Key Facts

A coal wholesaler challenged a decision issued by the Commission under the ECSC Treaty that it could not comply with and that it claimed would undermine its right to freely pursue its business activities which it in turn claimed was a breach of fundamental human rights guaranteed by the German constitution.

Key Law

The ECJ rejected the claim on the basis that the wholesaler was not being discriminated against since it was being treated no differently from other undertakings that also could not comply. However, it also stated that fundamental human rights form an integral part of the general principles of law that must be observed.

Key Judgment

The Court stated that in safeguarding such rights it was bound 'to draw inspiration from constitutional traditions common to the Member States, and . . . cannot therefore uphold measures which are incompatible . . . Similarly, international Treaties for the protection of human rights . . . of which they are signatories, can supply guidelines which should be followed'.

Key Link

Now the amended Art 11 in any case guarantees human rights:

1) The Union is founded on the principles of liberty, democracy, respect for human rights and fundamental freedoms, and the rule of law, principles which are common to the Member States.

2) The Union shall respect fundamental rights as guaranteed by the European Convention for the Protection of Human Rights and Fundamental Freedoms signed in Rome on 4 November 1950 and as they result from the constitutional traditions common to the Member States, as general principles of Community law.

4 Enforcement of EU law

Art 258 infringement proceedings against Member States

- Usually brought by Commission as watchdog.
- Three clear purposes:
    - i) to ensure Member States comply with Treaties;
    - ii) to provide a procedure for dispute resolution;
    - iii) to provide means of clarifying law.
- Starts with mediation, then three formal stages:
    - i) notice of default;
    - ii) reasoned opinion;
    - iii) proceedings in ECJ.
- Penalties possible in Art 260.
- An action by another state possible under Art 259 (*France v UK*).

ENFORCEMENT (DIRECT ACTIONS)

Art 263 actions against institutions for abuse of power:

- Two major functions:
    - i) provides way of controlling legality of binding acts;
    - ii) gives legal protection to those subject to Community instruments adversely affected by illegal ones.
- Commission, Council, Member States are privileged claimants.
- Natural and legal persons gain *locus standi* for a decision addressed to them or a regulation or a decision addressed to another person of direct and individual concern to them or against a regulatory act of direct concern to them and not entailing implementing measures.
- Individual concern means decision affects them because of attributes (*Plaumann v Commission*).
- A Regulation may be challenged if it has no general application but is a 'bundle of individual Decisions' (*International Fruit Co v Commission*).
- Grounds for review include: lack of competence, infringement of an essential procedural requirement, infringement of Treaties or procedural rules, misuse of powers.

Art 265 actions against institutions for failing to act:

- Can challenge Commission, Council, Parliament, European Central Bank.
- Privileged claimants are Member States and institutions.
- Natural and legal persons must show institution failed to address to them any instrument other than an opinion or recommendation.
- Grounds for review are where applicant can show he was entitled to a Decision and none was addressed to him, or an action has not been taken which is of direct and individual concern to him.

Art 340 actions for damages against institutions:

- 'To make good any damage caused by institutions.'
- Almost unrestricted *locus standi*.
- D must be an institution or its servant, not EU as a whole (*Werhahn Hansamuhle v Council*).
- Conditions for liability are:
    - i) damage suffered by claimant;
    - ii) fault of institution;
    - iii) causal connection.

▶ 4.1 Enforcement: introduction

1   Substantive rights and obligations granted under Treaties would be ineffective if left merely to the co-operation of Member States.

2   Individual rights may be abused by EU institutions and by Member States.

3   So, a variety of enforcement proceedings and methods for reviewing the actions of both institutions and Member States were created in the Treaty, placed under the scrutiny of the ECJ, with individuals able to gain remedies.

4   These procedures are known as 'direct actions' and supplement 'indirect actions' of the Art 267 reference procedure.

5   The measures are broad in that they allow a wide range of applicants to initiate proceedings.

▶ 4.2 Art 258 infringement proceedings against Member States

4.2.1 Introduction

1   EU law depends on a partnership with Member States, e.g. in the implementation of directives.

2   But it is not uncommon for Member States to be careless or even reluctant in fulfilling their obligations.

3   So the Treaty provides the means of calling Member States to account.

4   It is normally invoked by the Commission under Art 258.

5   But it can be initiated by other Member States under Art 259.

4.2.2 Actions by the Commission under Art 258

1   Commission is 'watchdog of Treaties' so is empowered by Art 258 to monitor behaviour of Member States and enforce compliance with Treaty obligations if necessary.

2   By Art 258: 'if Commission considers a member state has failed to fulfil an obligation . . . it shall deliver a reasoned opinion on the matter after giving state concerned opportunity to submit its observations. If state concerned does not comply . . . within period laid down [Commission] may bring matter before Court of Justice.'

3   So Art 258 has three clear purposes:
  ● to ensure Member States comply with Treaty obligations;
  ● to provide a procedure for dispute resolution;
  ● to provide means of clarifying law for all Member States.

4   There are three formal stages in the procedure – but these are usually preceded by an informal stage.
  ● Mediation (informal): the Commission engages in discussions with the Member State, which will usually remedy the error at this point. The action is then discontinued.
  ● Formal notice of default:
    i)   where the Commission remains dissatisfied it issues a notice inviting the Member State to submit its own observations;
    iii) this stage defines the terms of reference which are then fixed (*Commission v Italy (Re Payment of Export Rebates) 31/69*).
  ● Reasoned opinion:
    i)   issued if the Member State still fails to comply;
    ii) sets out reasons why the Member State is in default and a time limit;
    iii) but is not itself binding (*Alfonse Lutticke GmbH v Hauptzollamt Saarlouis 57/65*).
  ● Court proceedings in the ECJ:
    i)   the Commission brings an action if the Member State still fails to comply;
    ii) but the issue can still be settled without a court decision, e.g. interim relief under Art 279;
    iii) many defences have been tried, but most fail:
      a) internal difficulties (*Commission v Belgium 77/69*);
      b) reciprocity (*Commission v France (Re restrictions on lamb imports) 232/78*);
      c) *force majeure* (*Commission v Italy 101/84*);
      d) objections by trade unions (*Commission v UK 128/78*).

5   Enforcement:
  ● before TEU the ECJ's decisions were incapable of actual enforcement, so more Art 258 proceedings were used;
  ● now, by Art 260, a financial penalty is possible, e.g. *Commission v Greece* C-387/97 and this would particularly apply where there is a serious breach of EU law (*Commission v France* C-121/07).

4.2.3 Actions brought by Member States under Art 259

1   This was always intended to be an exceptional procedure.

2   However, it is a useful safeguard against errors of judgment by the Commission.

3   It is a similar procedure, though the Member State should work closely with the Commission in preliminary stages.

4   Only one case has been brought so far – *France v UK* 141/78.

▌ 4.3 Art 263 actions against Institutions for exceeding powers

4.3.1 Introduction

1   Art 263 is one of the few instances by which individuals can bring action in the ECJ, though their ability to do so is more restricted than for Institutions.

2   The procedure has two major functions:

   ● it provides a means of controlling the legality of binding acts of EU institutions;

   ● it gives legal protection to those subject to EU instruments adversely affected by illegal ones.

4.3.2 *Locus standi*

1   Member States, the Commission and the Council are all named in Art 263:

   ● so are all 'privileged claimants' with virtually unlimited rights of challenge (except for recommendations and opinions);

   ● provided the measure complained of has binding effect on the claimant.

2   Parliament and the European Central Bank are privileged claimants but with more limited powers of challenge. They may only bring an action 'for the purpose of protecting their prerogatives'.

3   Natural and legal persons also gain *locus standi* by Art 263, but rights of challenge are limited to 'a Decision addressed to that person, or a Decision which, although in the form of a Regulation or a Decision addressed to another person, is of direct and individual concern to the individual or against a regulatory act of direct concern to them and not entailing implementing measures . . .'.

4   So, except in the case of decisions addressed to the individual, there are three key issues to be established:

● What is individual concern?

   i)   The decision must affect the applicant 'by reason of certain attributes which are peculiar to them or by reason of circumstances in which they are differentiated from all other persons and by virtue of these factors distinguishes them individually just as . . . person addressed . . .' (*Plaumann v Commission 25/62*).

   ii) Since modified so that it must also be possible to determine the identity of persons affected at the time the measure complained of was adopted (*Toepfler v Commission* 106 and 107/63).

   iii) The ECJ has said there must be a 'closed group' of people affected (*International Fruit Co. v Commission 41–44/70*).

   iv) However, there is inconsistent application (*Piraiki-Patraiki v Commission* 11/82).

   v)   The AG in *UPA v Council C-50/00* suggested that a better test was: 'has the individual suffered a substantial adverse affect?' – but the ECJ confirmed *Plaumann* test in *Jego-Quere et cie v Commission* T-177/01.

● What is direct concern?

   i)   It is different from individual concern, but still subject to inconsistent interpretation.

   ii) As well as causal connection it refers to 'immediate, automatic and inevitable disadvantageous legal effects' without need for further intervention (*Alcan Aluminium Raeren et al v Commission 69/69*).

   iii) However, this strict standard has since been relaxed (*Bock v Commission 62/70 (The Chinese Mushrooms Case)*).

   iv) But direct concern involves affecting the legal situation of the person concerned, so members of political parties acting on their own behalf rather than the party's fail the test (*Bonde and Others v Parliament and Council* T-13/04; *Bonino and Others v Parliament and Council* T-40/04; *Front National and Others v Parliament and Council* C-486/01).

● When is a Regulation to be seen as a 'Decision affecting the applicant'?

   i)   Genuine Regulations are never capable of challenge by an individual (*Calpak SpA v Commission 789/79*).

   ii) So, a Regulation must fit the label given to it – *Confederation Nationale des Producteurs de Fruits et Legumes v Council* 16 and

17/72: 'what distinguishes a Regulation is not the greater or lesser extent of its application, material or territorial, but the fact that its provisions apply impersonally in objective situations . . .'

iii) So, a Regulation may be challenged when it has no general application but is 'a bundle of individual Decisions taken by the Commission, each of which, although taken in the form of a Regulation, affected the legal position of the applicant . . .' (*International Fruit Co. v Commission 41–44/70*).

4.3.3 Substantive grounds for review

1 Once admissibility is established the claimant must show that the challenge concerns one of four grounds identified in Article.

2 Lack of competence:

- there is no direct comparison in English law, but seen as comparable to the *ultra vires* doctrine;

- it occurs if an institution exercises a power not conferred upon it by EU law, or exercises a non-existent power, or encroaches on the power of another institution;

- the ECJ has defined the ground but will rarely accept challenges between institutions (*Commission v Council (Re European Road Transport Agreement) 22/70 (The ERTA case)*);

- so, it is more likely to be used for powers not possessed at all (*Ford (Europe) v Commission 228 and 229/82*);

- or often for improper delegation (*Meroni v High Authority 9/56*).

3 Infringement of an essential procedural requirement:

- EU law imposes procedural requirements as safeguards.

- Essential procedures include:

  i) preparation, e.g. prior consultation (*Roquette Freres v Council 138/79*);

  iii) communication giving reasons (*Germany v Commission 52 and 55/65*).

4 Infringement of Treaties or rules relating to their application:

- allows the ECJ to review whether the acts of the institutions conform to EU law;

- can include all aspects, e.g. general principles, so any sort of violation of EU law will be invalid (*Transocean Marine Paint Association v Commission 17/74*).

5   Misuse of powers:
   ● refers to an institution using a power it possesses but for objects contrary to those for which it was granted;
   ● may include any illegitimate use of power (*Bock v Commission* 62/70 *(The Chinese Mushrooms case)*).

4.3.4 Procedure

1   The most important requirement is a strict time limit for bringing an action.
2   This is two months from the date on which the measure was published, was notified to the claimant or came to his attention – but this may be extended if there are unforeseeable circumstances or *force majeure*.
3   The consequences of a successful claim is for the instrument to be declared void by the ECJ.

▶ 4.4 Art 265 actions against Institutions for a failure to act

4.4.1 General

1   Art 265 allows Member States and EU institutions to challenge the Council, Commission, Parliament and European Central Bank for not acting when they should.
2   It is the natural corollary of Art 263 proceedings.
3   Applicants must satisfy admissibility and show suitable grounds for review.

4.4.2 Admissibility

1   Three conditions must be met.
2   Title to sue (*locus standi*):
   ● 'privileged claimants' are 'Member States and other institutions', which now includes Parliament (*Parliament v Council* 377/87);
   ● 'natural and legal persons' can bring action against an institution which failed to address to that person any instrument other than a recommendation or an opinion.
3   It must be an indictable institution – the Council, Commission, Parliament or the Central Bank.
4   A prior approach to the institution:
   ● must be made by the applicant before applying to the ECJ;

- it must be explicit and refer to the possibility of Art 265 if no reply within two months.

4.4.3 Grounds for review

1   Will be where the applicant can show he was entitled to a decision and none was addressed to him, or an action has not been taken which is of direct and individual concern to him.

2   Few cases are admissible so there are few guidelines.

3   Generally, if there is a result to be achieved and an obligation is sufficiently well defined then any attempt to disregard it will fall within scope of Art 265 (*Parliament v Council 13/83*).

▶ 4.5 Art 340 actions for damages

4.5.1 General

1   Art 340 states: 'In the case of non-contractual liability, the EU shall . . . make good any damage caused by the Institutions or by its servants in the performance of their duties.'

2   So it is a general tort action but based more on French civil law.

4.5.2 Admissibility

1   *Locus standi* is almost unrestricted – any natural or legal person can claim provided the party him/herself has suffered damage resulting from an act or omission of an institution or its servant.

2   The defendant must be an institution or its servant, not the EU as a whole (*Werhahn Hansamuhle v Council 63–69/72*).

3   The appropriate time limit is five years from the date of the event giving rise to the action.

4.5.3 Conditions for liability

1   Three elements must be satisfied for a successful claim.

2   Damage suffered by the claimant:
   - can be any damage that is certain, provable and quantifiable;
   - future loss is recoverable in some circumstances (*Kampffmeyer et al v Commission 5,7 and 13–24/66*);
   - even highly speculative loss is recoverable in some circumstances (*Adams v Commission 145/83*).

3   Fault on the part of the institution complained of:

- it is only necessary to show that the claimant was owed a duty which was breached (*Adams v Commission* 145/83);

- but the ECJ is less likely to conclude fault where the institution makes policy decisions and errs (*Zuckerfabrik Schoppenstedt v Council* 5/71);

- although it has been established that liability is possible even in the absence of unlawful conduct (*FIAMM and FIAMM Technologies v Council and Commission* T-69/00) provided that there is unusual and special damage (*Galileo v Commission* T-279/03).

4   A causal connection between measure and damage:

- proof of damage alone is insufficient for liability without proof that the act of the institution directly caused it (*Dumortier Frères SA v Council* 27,28 and 45/79);

- so remoteness is an important factor (*Pool v Council* 49/79).

Key Cases Checklist

Art 258 Actions against Member States

Commission v Belgium (1970)
Liability arises whenever any state body fails to fulfil its obligations

Art 263 Actions against institutions for exceeding their powers

***Plaumann v Commission* (1963)**
Individual concern means that the decision affects the body because of attributes it has
***International Fruit Co. v Commission* (1971)**
A Regulation may be challenged if it has no general application but is a 'bundle of individual Decisions'

Enforcement (Direct Actions)

Art 265 Actions against institutions for failing to act

***Parliament v Council* (1987)**
Art 265 is applied where the applicant can show that they were entitled to a decision and none was actually addressed to them or an action has not been taken which is of direct and individual concern to them

Art 340 Actions for damages against institutions

***Zuckerfabrik Schoppenstedt v Council* (1971)**
• there must be a legislative measure which involves choices of economic policy
• and this must involve a breach of a superior rule of law
• which is sufficiently serious
• and the superior rule is of a type which was for the protection of individuals
• and only if all parts are satisfied can fault be shown

4.2.2

Commission v Belgium 77/69 [1970] ECR 237

Key Facts

Belgium had breached Art 95 (now Art 114 TFEU) by a discriminatory tax on wood. The Belgian Government argued that an amendment was actually put before its Parliament but never gained force because Parliament was dissolved in the meantime. It argued that, since it was prevented from legislating, the breach was beyond its control.

Key Law

The ECJ would not accept this reasoning and held that 'liability under [Art 258] arises whatever the agency of the State whose action or inaction is the cause of the failure to fulfill its obligations'.

4.3.2

Plaumann v Commission 25/62 [1963] ECR 95

Key Facts

German importers, including Plaumann, complained that a refusal by the Commission to suspend customs duties on mandarin oranges and tangerines exceeded its powers. Their argument failed when it was shown that any individual in Germany might have imported the fruit so they could not show 'individual concern'.

Key Law

It was held that in order for a private applicant to claim under [Art 258 TFEU] individual concern must be shown and this means that the decision or Regulation must affect the applicant.

Key Judgment

The court held that this would be 'by reason of certain attributes which are peculiar to them or by reason of circumstances in which they are differentiated from all other persons and by virtue of these factors distinguishes them individually just as in the case of the person addressed'.

Key Link

Töepfer v Commission 106 &107/63 [1965] ECR 405 which slightly modifies this; and see also *Bonde and Others v Parliament and Council* T-13/04 where Members of Parliament acting in their own name rather than their party's did not have direct concern.

4.3.2

International Fruit Co v Commission 41–44/70 [1971] ECR 411

Key Facts

A decision only applied to a limited number of importers who had been granted licenses before a specific date. The issue was whether the importers had *locus standi* to challenge the decision.

Key Law

The ECJ held that there will be individual concern and therefore *locus standi* is possible if there is a 'closed group' of people affected by the decision. In the case there was such a 'closed group' because of the limited number of importers.

Key Judgment

The Court stated that a Regulation can only be challenged when it is not one having general application within the meaning given in [Art 288 TFEU] but is instead 'a bundle of individual Decisions taken by the Commission, each of which, although taken in the form of a Regulation, affected the legal position of the applicant'.

4.3.2

Unión de Pequenos Agricultores (UPA) v Council C-50/00 [2003] QB 893

Key Facts

A trade association unsuccessfully challenged a Regulation in the CFI (now the General Court) as it could not show individual concern. The court stated that it could have brought an action instead in the national court and then asked for a reference. The case went on to the ECJ.

Key Law

The Advocate-General, in his reasoned opinion, stated that a challenge under [Art 263 TFEU] was a more appropriate procedure and acknowledged the inherent difficulties in trying to follow the route recommended by the CFI (now the General Court). A national court would not have the power to annul the measure and so could only consider whether there was enough doubt as to its legality to justify a reference being made. Also certain measures would not give rise to actions in national courts, so could not be challenged by individuals. He also felt the definition of individual concern was too restrictive and that there was no reason why an individual should have to show a difference from other individuals affected by the measure. He preferred a test based on an individual having suffered a substantial adverse affect because of his particular circumstances. Nevertheless, the ECJ confirmed the *Plaumann* (1963) test.

Key Link

Quere et Cie v Commission T–177/01 [2003] QB 854, where between the Advocate-General's opinion and the ECJ ruling in *UPA* the CFI (now the General Court) suggested a different test based on the Advocate-General's opinion in *UPA*. There would be individual concern if the measure 'affects his legal position in a manner which is both definite and immediate, by restricting his rights or imposing obligations on him'.

Key Problem

The result is that there is unlikely to be any change to the definition now without amendment to the Treaty.

4.3.2   *Ford (Europe) v Commission* 228 and 229/82 [1984] ECR 1129

Key Facts

Ford challenged an interim decision by the Commission on Ford's ban on selling right-hand drive Ford vehicles to dealers in Germany.

Key Law

The ECJ held that a challenge was possible because the Commission had no power to make interim decisions.

Key Comment

This suggests that it is probably easier for Art 263 TFEU to be used in respect of powers that are not possessed at all by the institution challenged in the application than where powers are simply abused.

4.3.4 *Transocean Marine Paint Association v Commission* 17/74 [1975] 2 CMLR D75

Key Facts

The Association had enjoyed an exemption from Art 85 (now Art 101 TFEU) for ten years when the Commission unilaterally reviewed the exemption and imposed entirely new conditions.

Key Law

The Court held that the Commission had acted in breach of a general right to be heard, and of the general principle of legal certainty. Its act was thus invalid.

Key Comment

The ground allows the ECJ to review how the acts of the institutions conform to EU law. As this includes the general principles any violation of EU law of any type may be declared invalid.

4.3.2 *Werner A. Bock KG v Commission (the Chinese Mushrooms case)* 62/70 [1971] ECR 897

Key Facts

A firm applied to import Chinese mushrooms into Germany. Since the mushrooms were freely available in the EC (now EU) at the time, the German Government needed authority from the Commission if it wished to prohibit the import. The Commission issued a decision allowing the import ban.

Key Law

The ECJ decided that the import ban lacked proportionality but also considered the question of misuse of power by the Commission and held that there was evidence of collaboration between the Commission and the German Government in the issuing of the decision so that there was a misuse of power. The Commission used its power to issue decisions, a power that it does in fact possess, but did so for an objective that was contrary to what it was given for and the decision was invalid.

4.4.3   *Parliament v Council* 13/83 [1987] ECR 1513

Key Facts

This involved a challenge by Parliament over an alleged failure by the Council: i) to ensure freedom to provide international transport; and ii) to establish the conditions in which non-resident transporters were able to operate in other Member States.

Key Law

The Court accepted this as an appropriate ground for review and identified that [Art 265 TFEU] is appropriate where the applicant can show that they were entitled to a decision and none was actually addressed to them or where an action has not been taken which is of direct and individual concern to them. The Court held that the Council had failed on the second count because it involved a legally perfect obligation which should have been implemented within the transitional period. It did not accept the first count because it was too imprecise. However, the case has subsequently led to development of an EC (now EU) transport policy.

Key Problem

There are no clear guidelines on when Art 265 TFEU actions are appropriate. However, generally if there is a result to be achieved and an obligation is sufficiently well defined then any attempt to disregard it will fall within the scope of an Art 265 TFEU action.

4.5.3

Zuckerfabrik Schoppenstedt v Council 5/71 [1971] ECR 975

Key Facts

A Regulation laid down measures to offset the differences between national sugar prices and Community (now EU) reference prices that were applicable from a particular date. The applicant complained that the criteria were in fact erroneous and had caused him loss.

Key Law

The applicant failed in his complaint since the Court held that the Community (now EU) will not incur liability for a legislative measure that involves choices of economic policy unless there has been a breach of a superior rule of law for the protection of individuals. The ECJ also laid down criteria for determining fault (the so-called '*Schoppenstedt* formula'):

- there must be a legislative measure which involves choices of economic policy;
- and this must involve a breach of a superior rule of law;
- which is sufficiently serious;
- and the superior rule is of a type which was for the protection of individuals;
- and only if all parts are satisied will fault be shown.

Key Comment

There are three elements required for a successful claim:

- damage suffered by the applicant;
- fault on the part of the institution complained about;
- a causal connection between the measure complained of and the damage suffered.

Key Link

Adams v Commission 145/83 [1985] ECR 3539, where the applicant's wife hanged herself when he was arrested for industrial espionage and this was accepted as recoverable damage.

5 The relationship between EU law and national law

Supremacy:

- Vital to ensure supranational character of institutions, but not mentioned in Treaties.
- First stated in *Van Gend en Loos* – states have given up sovereignty to new legal order.
- Explained in *Costa v ENEL* – clear limitation of sovereign right upon which subsequent unilateral law, incompatible with aims of EU, cannot prevail.
- Any conflict is settled in favour of EU law (*Simmenthal*).
- Following *R v Secretary of State for Transport, ex parte Factortame No (2)* national court can do everything necessary to set aside national legislative provisions which might prevent [EU] rules from having full force and effect.

EU LAW AND NATIONAL LAW

Art 267 References:

- Means of ensuring uniform applications of EU law.
- Any court may refer – some have mandatory referral.
- ECJ test in CILFIT of where reference unnecessary: where EU law irrelevant or peripheral; or where there is an existing interpretation; or where correct interpretation is so obvious that no doubt exists.
- *Foglia v Novello*: reference must involve genuine issue of EU law; and will genuinely assist national court to make a judgment; but cannot be used merely to test the law or to delay the case.

Direct applicability

- Measure becomes part of national law without further enactment.
- So applies to Regulations but not to directives.

Direct effect:

- *Van Gend en Loos v Nederlands Administratie der Belastingen* accepted that certain measures should be enforceable by citizens of Member States – if they were clear, precise and unconditional, and conferred rights on individuals;
- this is straightforward in the case of substantive Treaty Articles – *Reyners v Belgium*;
- and even in the case of decisions – *Grad v Finanzamt Traustein*;
- but not for directives which are not a complete legal instrument.

Direct effect of directives:

- *Van Duyn v Home Office* recognised that it would be incompatible with the binding nature of a directive in Art 288 if they could not be enforced;
- so provided that the date for implementation is passed – *Pubblico Ministero v Ratti*;
- they may be 'vertically' directly effective against the state itself – *Marshall v Southampton and SW Hampshire AHA (No 1)*;
- or an 'emanation of the state' – *Foster v British Gas plc*.

Indirect effect:

- *Von Colson and Kamann v Land Nordrhein-Westfalen* allows that since Member States have an obligation formerly under Art 10 (now Art 4(3) TEU) to give full effect to EU law then they should interpret an improperly implemented directive so as to give effect to its objectives.

State liability:

- *Brasserie/Factortame* provides an action against states for failure to implement directives where the citizen suffers loss as a result.

▶ 5.1 Supremacy of EU law

5.1.1 The reasons for the doctrine of supremacy

1   Supremacy has become:
   ● the most entrenched; and
   ● probably the least contested of EU principles.

2   It is essential that EU law should be uniformly applied.

3   Without 'supremacy' there could be no supranational context for the institutions, which would then have no effective power.

4   So, the real justifications for supremacy are:
   ● the prevention of any questioning of the validity of EU law in Member States.
   ● the doctrine of 'pre-emption':
      i)   prevention of alternative legal interpretations of EU law by Member State courts;
      ii) prevention of enactment of conflicting legislation by Member State governments.

5   However, the Treaties themselves make no reference to supremacy over all national law. The closest is the former Art 10 (the duty of loyalty) (now in Art 4(3) TEU): 'Member States shall take all appropriate measures . . . to ensure fulfilment of the obligations arising out of this Treaty or resulting from actions taken by the institutions . . . They shall abstain from any measure which could jeopardise the attainment of the objectives of the Treaty . . .'. This has become a major tool in the hands of the ECJ.

6   Ultimately, the most logical basis for supremacy is the requirement of full integration. In any case economic integration would be virtually impossible if Member States could deny and defy the supranational powers of the institutions.

5.1.2 The early statements of supremacy

1   The earliest definition of supremacy is in 26/62 *Van Gend en Loos v The Commission*: 'The [EU] constitutes a new legal order in international law, for whose benefits the states have limited their sovereign rights, albeit within limited fields . . .'

2   The key effect of supremacy, then, is to limit the ability of Member States to legislate contrary to EU law.

3   The definitive explanation came in 6/64 *Costa v ENEL*: 'By contrast with ordinary international treaties, the EEC Treaty has created its own legal system which on entry into force . . . became an integral part of the legal systems of the Member States and which their courts are bound to apply . . . The transfer by Member States from their national orders in favour of the [EU] order . . . carries with it a clear limitation of their sovereign right upon which a subsequent unilateral law, incompatible with the aims of the [EU]cannot prevail . . .'

4   Three points clearly emerge:

● Member States have given up certain of their sovereign powers to make law;

● Member States and their citizens are bound by EU law;

● Member States cannot unilaterally introduce conflicting law.

5   The ECJ has also declared that EU law cannot be invalidated even by national constitutional law – *International Handelsgesellschaft v EVGF* 11/70: 'Recourse to the legal rules or concepts of national law in order to judge the validity of measures adopted by the institutions . . . would have an adverse effect on the uniformity and efficacy of [EU] law. The validity of such measures can only be judged in the light of [EU]law . . .'

6   So the ECJ has insisted that where EU law and national law conflict a court must give effect to the EU law – *Simmenthal SpA* 106/77: 'the relationship between the provisions of the Treaty and directly applicable measures of the institutions on the one hand and national law . . . on the other . . . render automatically inapplicable any conflicting provision of current national law but . . . also preclude the valid adoption of new national legislative measures to the extent that they would be incompatible with [EU] provisions . . . every national court must . . . apply [EU] law in its entirety . . . and must accordingly set aside any provision of national law which may conflict with it whether prior or subsequent . . .'

7   Supremacy applies not only to directly conflicting national law, but to any contradictory law which encroaches on an area of EU competence (*Commission v France (The Merchant Sailor's case)* 167/73).

5.1.3 Continued development of the doctrine

1   The ECJ has continued to modify and expand the principle.

2   Another far-reaching statement allowed national courts to set aside national legislation in areas of conflict – *R v Secretary of State for Transport, ex parte Factortame No (2)* C-213/89: 'any legislative, administrative, or judicial practice which might impair the effectiveness of [the EU] by withholding from the national court . . . the power to do everything necessary . . . to set aside national legislative provisions which might prevent . . . [EU] rules from having full force and effect are incompatible with those requirements which are the very essence of [EU] law . . . the full effectiveness of [EU] law would be just as much impaired if a rule of national law could prevent a court . . . from granting interim relief . . . It therefore follows that a court which . . . would grant interim relief, if it were not for a rule of national law, is obliged to set aside
that law . . .'

3   The ECJ has also developed the principle that courts must interpret national legislation to comply with EU obligations, whether national law precedes or follows the conflicting EU law (*Von Colson v Land Nordrhein-Westfalen* 14/83, further developed by *Marleasing v La Comercial* 106/89).

4   The principle of liability towards citizens who suffer loss from a Member State's breach of EU law also extends the doctrine of supremacy (*Francovich v Italy* 6/90 and 9/90).

5.1.4 Responses to supremacy by Member States

1   Different states have responded in different ways.

2   Belgium and supremacy:

   ● a monist state in respect of the international Treaty;

   ● but EU law was incorporated by statute, so some early doubts on supremacy;

   ● issue settled in *Minister for Economic Affairs v Fromagerie Franco-Suisse 'Le Ski'* (1972) – usual rule that a later statute repeals an earlier one could not apply to EU law, so EU law was supreme.

3   France and supremacy:

   ● differences have occurred between civil appeal court views and the administrative court (*Conseil d'Etat*);

   ● civil courts have always accepted that EU law prevails over inconsistent cases and statute (*Von Kempis v Geldof* (1976));

- but *Conseil d'Etat* has held that Directives cannot be used to challenge national administrative law (*Minister for the Interior v Cohn Bendit* (1980));

- though recently more prone to accept the principle.

4 Italy and supremacy:

- takes a 'constructionist' approach – Italian law construed to be consistent with EU law;

- the leading case is *Frontini* (1974): EU law is separate and superior and not within the scope of review of the Italian constitutional court.

5 Germany and supremacy:

- originally favoured constitution over EU because of human rights (*International Handelsgessellschaft* (1970));

- but supremacy accepted if human rights were upheld (*Wunsche Handelsgesselschaft* (1987));

- but is still prone to argue for national sovereignty (*Brunner* (1994)).

6 UK and supremacy:

- In the UK the focus has always been on interpretation of the EC Act 1972.

- Section 2(1) gives force to EU law: 'All such rights, powers, liabilities, obligations and restrictions . . . created or arising by or under the Treaties, are without further enactment to be given legal effect . . .'

- Supremacy appears to be guaranteed by s 2(4) which provides: '. . . any enactment passed or to be passed . . . shall be construed and have effect subject to the foregoing provision of this section . . .'

- Traditional argument has centred on whether it is an entrenched principle or merely a rule of construction.

- Judges have been willingly liberal in taking the latter view (*Garland v British Rail Engineering Ltd* (1979)).

- Judges have advocated a purposive approach to interpretation (*Pickstone v Freeman* (1988) and *Litster v Forth Dry Dock Co* (1989)).

- However, in *Duke v Reliance GEC* (1988) Lord Templeman suggested that s 2(4) does not permit an English court to 'distort a statute to enforce a Directive which has no direct effect between individuals . . .'

- On Parliament's ability to deliberately oppose the EU, Lord Denning's view was: 'if . . . Parliament deliberately passes an Act with the intention of repudiating the Treaty or any provisions in it . . . and says so in express terms, then I would have thought that it would be the duty of our courts to follow the statute of our Parliament . . .' (*Macarthys v Smith* 129/79) – so ECA 1972 cannot be impliedly repealed though express repeal is theoretically retained.

- But acceptance of supremacy is now more clearly stated – Hoffman J in *Stoke-on-Trent v B and Q plc* (1990): 'The . . . Treaty is the supreme law of the UK taking precedence over Acts of Parliament. Entry into the [EU] meant that Parliament surrendered its sovereign right to legislate contrary to the provisions of the Treaty . . . partial surrender of sovereignty was more than compensated for by the advantages of membership . . .'

- And the definitive view of the meaning and scope of the 1972 Act is now Lord Bridge's in *Factortame*: '. . . whatever limitations of its sovereignty Parliament accepted when it enacted the EC Act 1972 was entirely voluntary. Under the terms of the 1972 Act it has always been clear that it is the duty of a UK court, when delivering final judgement, to override any rule of national law found to be in conflict with any directly enforceable rule of [EU] law . . .'

▶ 5.2 Direct applicability and direct effect

5.2.1 Introduction

1   With supremacy, direct effect is another major element in ensuring the application of EU law in the Member States.

2   It must be distinguished from direct applicability – Art 288 refers to certain EU measures being either generally applicable or directly applicable.

3   The three are distinguished as follows:

- general applicability merely means that the measure applies throughout the whole EU (so it would apply to a regulation but not to a decision);

- direct applicability means that the measure becomes part of national law without need for further enactment (so it would apply to a regulation but not to a directive);

- direct effect means that the measure creates rights and obligations which are enforceable in the national courts as well as in the ECJ (so it could easily apply to Treaty Articles and regulations, but is more problematic when applied to directives).

4   So there is a distinction between these last two:

- directly applicable measures need not create justiciable rights, e.g. a procedural regulation;

- direct effect can exist without direct applicability, e.g. a Directive;

- but a measure could be both.

5   Direct effect has been described as 'the first step in the judicial contribution to federalism . . .' (P. Craig: *Once Upon a Time in the West* (1992) 12 OJLS 453).

6   It has also been described as 'a second principle of western jurisprudence to run alongside supremacy; namely the rule of law . . .' (Ian Ward: *A Critical Introduction to European Law*, CUP).

7   Its most powerful justification is that it 'enhances the effectiveness or *effet utile* of binding norms of [EU] law . . .' (Josephine Shaw: *Law of the European Union*, Palgrave).

8   It is the creation of the ECJ – its uncompromising nature has resulted in conflict with Member States and in turn even more uncompromising principles, such as indirect effect.

5.2.2 The basic requirements for direct effect

1   The principle was first accepted by the ECJ in *Van Gend en Loos v Nederlands Administratie der Belastingen* 26/62: '[EU] law . . . not only imposes obligations on individuals but is also intended to confer upon them rights which become part of their legal heritage. These rights are granted not only where they are expressly granted by the Treaty, but also by reason of obligations which the Treaty imposes in a clearly defined way upon individuals as well as upon Member States and the institutions of the [EU] . . .'

2   So the ECJ accepted that since the Treaty was clearly intended to affect individuals as well as Member States, it must be capable of creating rights which were enforceable by individuals.

3   The ECJ held that since Art 25 (now Art 30 TFEU) 'contains a clear and unconditional prohibition . . . it [is] ideally adapted to produce direct effects between Member States and their subjects . . .'

4   By *Van Gend en Loos* direct effect only applied to 'stand still Articles':

- but this limitation soon disappeared;

- and a variety of provisions have since been held to be directly effective;

● though there are still measures which remain unenforceable if worded in conditional terms.

5   The requirements for direct effect have been modified by the case law, e.g. *Reyner v Belgium* 2/74, and are: the provision must be clear, precise and unconditional and non-dependent.

6   *Van Gend en Loos* concerned a Treaty Article that conferred rights, but the principle of direct effect has been extended to other EU law by the case law.

5.2.3 The basic distinction between vertical and horizontal direct effect

1   The ECJ has also been responsible for helping to identify the principles of vertical and horizontal direct effect and clarifying the distinctions between them.

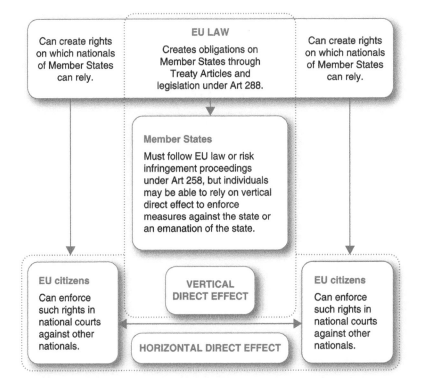

The differences between vertical and horizontal direct effect

2   The distinction can be critical in determining whether a person can enforce EU law in a national court.

3   Vertical direct effect concerns the relationship between EU law and the national law:

- measures of EU law create obligations on the state;

- so failure to honour such obligations would normally result in Art 258 action;

- but it can also mean that an individual can rely on the measures in an action against the state;

- this was the case in both *Van Duyn v Home Office* 41/74 and *Pubblico Ministero v Ratti* 148/78, which were both fought against government departments;

- the concept has been extended to include bodies that are 'emanations of the state' (public bodies) and so may extend rights to certain individuals.

4   Horizontal direct effect, on the other hand, is precisely about the relationship between individuals, so concerns rights enforceable in national courts.

5.2.4 Direct effect and Treaty articles

1   Direct effect was first accepted in *Van Gend en Loos*.

2   However, the principal test for application now is that laid down in *Reyners v Belgium* 2/74.

3   Directly effective Treaty Articles could include:

- 'stand still' Articles, e.g. *Van Gend en Loos* and Art 30 (then Art 25);

- originally also included Articles imposing a duty on the state to act, e.g. *Eunomia* 18/71 on Art 16 (now repealed);

- Articles that give rights to individuals, e.g. *Van Duyn v Home Office* 41/74 and Art 45; *Reyners v Belgium* 2/74 and Art 49; *Defrenne v SABENA* 43/75 and Art 157.

5.2.5 Direct effect and Regulations

1   Regulations create obligations without need for further enactment because they are of 'general application' and are 'directly applicable'.

2 So they will usually be directly effective, subject to *Reyners* test (*Leonesio v Ministero dell'Agricoltora and delle Foreste* 93/71 *(The widow Leonesio)*).

3 But a Regulation may not be directly effective if too vague.

5.2.6 Direct effect and Decisions

1 A decision by Art 288 is 'binding in its entirety on the party to whom it is addressed'.

2 So it would be 'incompatible with the binding nature of decisions to exclude the possibility of direct effect . . .' (*Grad v Finanzamt Traustein* 9/70).

3 It is less certain whether a decision addressed to a Member State could have horizontal effect.

5.2.7 Direct effect and Directives

1 By Art 288, directives are 'binding as to the result to be achieved':

- so they are seen as creating an obligation on Member States to pass law to achieve the objective;

- but not as automatically creating substantive rights for citizens to enforce, because they fail the *Van Gend* test – they are dependent.

2 The ECJ was prepared to overlook this limitation in *Van Duyn v Home Office*:

- because 'it would be incompatible with the binding effect attributed to a Directive by [Art 288] to exclude, in principle, the possibility that the obligation which it imposes may be invoked by those concerned . . .';

- so a directive can be enforced (but only vertically) provided that the criteria for direct effect are met (except the non-dependency rule).

3 But only where the time-limit for implementation has passed (*Pubblico Ministero v Ratti* 148/78).

4 Also, a directive can be vertically directly effective but never horizontally directly effective (*Marshall v Southampton and South West Hampshire AHA (Teaching) (No 1)* 152/84).

5 Where the directive is properly implemented there would be national law and so need to use direct effect. An unimplemented directive can only be relied on as against the state, e.g.:

- pre-privatised British Gas (*Foster v British Gas plc* 188/89); tax authorities (*Becker* 8/81); and the police (*Johnston v The Royal Ulster Constabulary* 222/84);

- but not a publicly owned manufacturing company (*Rolls Royce plc v Doughty* (1987));

- the test in *Foster* and also in *Griffin v South West Water* (1995) is whether:

  i)   the body provides a public service;

  ii) the body is under the control of the state;

  iii) the body exercises special powers;

- so this creates major anomalies in the case of private bodies (*Duke v Reliance GCE* (1988)), against whom an unimplemented directive cannot be enforced.

6   A directive can be referred to after implementation to ensure its objectives are achieved: *Verbond v Nederlands Ondernemingen* 51/76.

5.2.8 Indirect effect

1   As a result of the limitations of using vertical direct effect, the ECJ has used the obligation under the former Art 10 (now Art 4(3) TEU) to conform with and give effect to EU law (irrespective of whether or not it is directly effective) to develop the principle of indirect effect (the *Von Colson* principle), which applies to all EU law, not just directives.

2   As the court said in *Von Colson and Kamann v Land Nordrhein-Westfalen* 14/83, 'Since the duty under [Art 4(3) TEU] to ensure fulfilment of (an) obligation was binding on all national courts . . . it follows that . . . courts are required to interpret their national law in the light of the wording and purpose of the directive . . .'

3   The ECJ in *Von Colson* ignored the horizontal/vertical issue, and direct effect generally:

- it was left ambiguous as to which national law indirect effect would apply so, for example, the then HL refused to apply it in *Duke*;

- it was also left ambiguous how far national courts should go to ensure conformity of national law and EU law.

4   However, these problems seem to have been resolved by *Marleasing SA v La Comercial Internacional de Alimentacion* C-106/89:

- the ECJ held that the obligation to conform applied 'whether the provisions concerned pre-date or post-date the directive . . .';

- so its scope in *Marleasing* is potentially very wide, with consequences for precedent and statutory interpretation;

- although there does seem to be a difference between the *Von Colson* approach (to do 'everything possible' to achieve conformity), and the *Simmenthal* approach (to do 'everything necessary');

- the ECJ already seems to have linked the concepts of direct and indirect effect (*Johnston v Chief Constable of the RUC* 222/84).

5.2.9 State liability for failure to implement

1 The third way to avoid the problems of direct effect and directives came in *Francovich v Italy* 6/90 and 9/90:

- the ECJ held that 'the full effectiveness of [EU] provisions . . . and the rights they recognise would be undermined if individuals were unable to recover damages where their rights were infringed by a breach of [EU] law attributable to a member state . . .';

- so citizens should be able to sue the state for non-implementation of a directive.

2 The conditions for liability are:

- the directive must confer rights for individuals – the contents of which must be identifiable in the wording;

- there must be a causal link between the damage suffered and the failure to implement the directive;

- and the cases of *Brasserie du Pêcheur SA v Germany* and *R v Secretary of State for Transport, ex parte Factortame* 46 and 48/93 have added another – that the breach by the Member State is sufficiently serious;

- *Dillenkofer v Federal Republic of Germany* C-178/94 suggests that non-implementation is sufficiently serious so this is like strict liability;

- for other breaches, must show the breach was sufficiently serious (*R v Minister of Agriculture, Fisheries and Food ex parte Hedley Lomas* C-5/94).

3 The *Francovich* principle is the most far reaching and has several implications:

- it conflicts with national rules on non-implementation;

- but the need to show direct effect is removed;

- as is the strained construction of national law through indirect effect;

- it focuses instead on the duty of the Member State to implement EU law and attaches rigorous sanctions for failure to implement;

- so it removes any advantage of non-implementation.

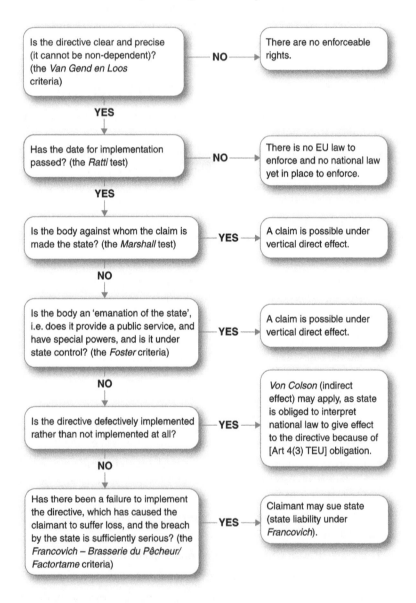

The possible enforceability of directives

▶ 5.3 Art 267 references and preliminary rulings

5.3.1 Introduction

1   Reference procedure is critical to both supremacy and direct effect, because it is the means of ensuring uniform application of the law.

2   The ethos of reference procedure is:

*   to create a collaborative bond between EU and the national courts;
*   to recognise that national courts are ultimately the best equipped to give effect to EU law;
*   to demonstrate that EU law is part of national law.

3   'The grand objectives of a [EU] legal order which include the intermeshing of [EU] law and national law, could not be achieved without some organic mechanism for ensuring the uniform application of [EU] law . . . the ECJ frequently reminds us that (this) is the purpose of Art [267 TFEU] . . .' (Josephine Shaw, *Law of the European Union*, Palgrave).

4   It provides a means for national courts to be guided on 'meaning or validity' of EU law in a case depending on EU law.

5   It accounts for the largest area of ECJ work, and for most of the crucially important decisions.

5.3.2 The scope of the Art 267 procedure

1   Under Art 267(1), as amended by the TEU, the ECJ has jurisdiction to give preliminary rulings on:

*   the interpretation of the TFEU;
*   the validity and interpretation of acts of EU Institutions (including the Central Bank).

2   So the ECJ clearly has jurisdiction to interpret all Treaty Articles and the acts of the Institutions, which are clearly those in Art 288: Regulations, Directives and Decisions.

3   The ECJ has no jurisdiction to interpret national law. But sometimes it has reformulated the question to better assist the national court (*Marks & Spencer v Customs and Excise Commissioners* C-62/00).

4   By Art 267(2), 'Where such a question is raised before any court or tribunal of a member state . . . [it] may, if it considers a decision on the question is necessary to enable it to give judgement, request the Court of Justice to give a ruling . . .'

5   By Art 267(3), 'Where any such question is raised in a case pending before a court or tribunal of a member state, against whose decisions there is no judicial remedy under national law, that court or tribunal shall bring the matter before the Court of Justice'.

5.3.3 The meaning of 'any court or tribunal'

1   This may include 'the whole range of bodies which embody the judicial power of the state regardless of what they are called . . .'

2   The key elements according to the ECJ in *Dorsch Consult* C-54/96 are that the body:

  ● must be recognised in the national judicial system;
  ● must be a permanent body;
  ● must exercise a judicial function;
  ● must give a decision according to the rule of law.

3   Examples of bodies falling within Art 267 procedure include:

  ● *Vaassen* 61/65, a Dutch Social Security Tribunal for migrant workers;
  ● *Broeckmeuler* 246/80, a Dutch GP's Registration Appeals Committee;
  ● *Pretore di Salo v X* 14/86, preliminary enquiries by a Magistrate;
  ● *Abrahamsson v Andersson* C-407/98, the Swedish Universities Appeal Board;
  ● *Korhonen* C-18/01, the Finnish Competition Council;
  ● in the UK it has included Employment Tribunals, the EAT and Social Security Tribunals and more recently a Special Commissioners of Income Tax (*Cadbury Schweppes* C-196/04).

4   Examples of bodies not within the scope of Art 267 include:

  ● *Borker* 138/80, the Paris Bar Council;
  ● *Nordsee Hochseefischerei GmbH v Reederei Mond* 102/81 and *Denuit & Cordenier* C-125/04, commercial arbitration;
  ● *Saltzman* C-78/99, a District Court acting as a Land Registry;
  ● *Lutz* C-182/00, a Regional Court acting as a Companies Registry.

5.3.4 Paragraph 2 and the discretion to refer

1   Paragraph 2 and paragraph 3 identify two different situations:

  ● discretionary referral – from the word 'may' in 2;
  ● mandatory referral – from the word 'shall' in 3.

2   By paragraph 2 courts have discretion to refer where they feel it is 'necessary'.

3   A national court will find it necessary when it requires an ECJ ruling in order to be able to give judgment.

4   The ECJ has developed its own test, in CILFIT 283/81, of when a reference is not necessary:

● where EU law is irrelevant or peripheral to the issue;

● where there is an existing interpretation – the principle of *acte clair* applies (see *Procureur de la Republique v Chiron* 271/84 and 274/84);

● where correct interpretation is so obvious that there can be no doubt.

5   UK courts have also drawn up their own guidelines:

● Lord Denning in *Bulmer v Bollinger* (1974) – before referring, the judge must be sure:

i)   EU law would be conclusive of the case;

ii) there is no previous ECJ ruling;

iii) the doctrine of *acte clair* does not apply;

iv) the facts of the case are already decided;

v)   delay caused by reference is not unwarranted;

● though these guidelines have been criticised for being too negative.

● A more positive approach is Bingham J in *Commissioners of Customs and Excise v Samex SpA* (1983) – the ECJ is better to interpret EU law because:

i)   it scrutinises all the language versions;

ii) it oversees EU law in total;

iii) it has a better understanding of purposive interpretation.

5.3.5 Paragraph 3 and the obligation to refer

1   This is known as the 'compulsory reference' procedure – strangely as there is much controversy surrounding when it will apply.

2   One view is that only courts of last resort are covered, e.g. Supreme Court in the UK.

3   But another view is that it includes any court where the right to appeal is denied for whatever reasons, e.g. in *Costa v ENEL* the reference was made by a *giudice conciliatore* (an Italian magistrate).

4   The position is very unsettled in the UK courts, e.g. see CA in *R v Henn and Darby* (1978) and the High Court in *Magnavision NV v General Optical Council (No 2)* (1987).

5   In general the risk of the 'floodgates' being opened seems to suggest that the strict meaning of paragraph 3 is compromised for the CILFIT criteria.

6   However, failure by a court of last resort to refer can result in an Art 258 action against the Member State.

5.3.6 The limitations on making references

1   These were stated in *Foglia v Novello (No 1) 104/79 and (No 2) 244/80*:

  ● reference must involve a genuine issue of EU law;

  ● reference will genuinely assist a national court to make a judgment;

  ● reference may not be used to give opinions on hypothetical situations in order to merely test the law;

  ● nor can a party merely use it as a delaying tactic;

  ● in these last two situations a reference will be refused.

2   The reference must be 'necessary'.

3   Only the ECJ has authority to declare provisions of EU law invalid – to prevent damaging uniform application of EU law: *Firma Foto-Frost v Hauptzollampt Lubeck 314/85*.

  ● So where a question is on validity of secondary legislation, reference must be made to *R (on application of BAT) v Secretary of State for Health* C-491/01.

5.3.7 The effect of preliminary ruling under Art 267

1   There is nothing specific in the Treaty to indicate what the effect will be.

2   However, it is clear that Member State courts are bound to decide cases in accordance with ECJ case law.

3   The ECJ has its own case law on the subject, suggesting that in a case where a reference has been made the ruling is binding on the national court (*Milch-Fett-und Eierkontor v HZA Saarbrucker 29/68*) (but the English High Court refused to apply preliminary ruling in *Arsenal FC v Reed* C-206/01, although this was reversed by the CA).

4   Though it is the interpretation of law which is binding – there is no question of *res judicata* applying.

Key Cases Checklist

Supremacy

***Van Gend en Loos* (1963)**
First statement – states have given up sovereignty to new legal order
***Costa v ENEL* (1964)**
Clear limitation of sovereign right upon which subsequent unilateral law,
incompatible with aims of EU cannot prevail
***International Handelsgessellschaft* (1970)**
Applies equally to national constitutional law
***R v Secretary of State for Transport ex p Factortame (No 2)* (1996)**
A national court can do everything necessary to set aside national legislative
provisions which might prevent EU rules from having full force and effect including
temporarily suspending operation of an Act of Parliament

Supremacy and Direct Effect

Direct effect
***Van Gend en Loos v Nederlands Administratie der Belastingen* (1963)**
Measures can be enforced if clear, precise and unconditional, and conferred rights
***Van Gend en Loos* (1963)** applies straightforwardly to substantive Treaty Articles;
***Leonesio v Ministero dell'Agricoltora & delle Foreste* (1972)** and to regulations;
***Grad v Finanzamt Traustein* (1970)** and decisions
Direct effect of directives
***Van Duyn v Home Office* (1974)**
Recognised that it would be incompatible with the binding nature of a directive in
Art 288 if they could not be enforced
***Pubblico Ministero v Ratti* (1979)**
But date for implementation must have passed
***Marshall v Southampton and S W Hampshire AHA (No 1)* (1986)**
May only be 'vertically' directly effective against the state itself
***Foster v British Gas plc* (1990)**
Or an 'emanation of the state' (provides public service, under state control, special
powers)
Indirect effect
***Von Colson and Kamann v Land Nordrhein-Westfalen* (1984)**
Since Member States have an obligation under formerly Art 10 (now Art 4(3) TEU)
to give full effect to EU law then they should interpret an improperly implemented
directive so as to give effect to its objectives
State liability
***Brasserie/Factortame* (1996)**
Can sue state for failure to implement directives if clearly gives right, breach is
sufficiently serious, and the citizen suffers loss caused by the breach of EU law

The meaning of 'court or tribunal'

***Broekmeulen v Huisarts Registratie Commissie* (1981)**
The ECJ applies a 'functionalist' rather than a 'literalist' test

Inadmissible references

***Foglia v Novello* (1981)**
Reference must involve genuine issue of EU law; and will genuinely assist national court to make a judgment; but cannot use to merely test the law or to delay the case

Art 267 References

References challenging the validity of EU law

***R (on the application of British American Tobacco) v Secretary of State for Health* (2003)**
The fact that a Directive is issued under an inappropriate Treaty Article need not affect its validity

Mandatory and discretionary references

***CILFIT Srl v Ministero della Sanita* (1982)**
A reference is not necessary: where EU law is irrelevant or peripheral; or there is an existing interpretation; or correct interpretation is so obvious that there can be no doubt

5.1.2   *Costa v ENEL* 6/64 [1964] ECR 585

Key Facts

Costa, a lawyer, owned shares in a pre-privatised Italian electric company and argued that the law privatising the industry was unlawful as it contravened [EU] law on monopolies. The Italian Government, after a judgment by the Italian constitutional court, argued that the proceedings themselves were unlawful since the Italian court should have followed the Italian law nationalising the electric industry which came after that ratifying the Treaty.

Key Law

The ECJ held that [EU] law took precedence over inconsistent national law, even that introduced after the signing of the Treaty.

Key Judgment

The court stated: 'By contrast with ordinary international treaties, the EC Treaty [now TFEU] has created its own legal system which on entry into force ... became an integral part of the legal systems of the member states and which their courts are bound to apply ... the member states have limited their sovereign rights ... and have thus created a body of law which binds both their nationals and themselves.' And, on the consequences: 'The transfer, by member states from their national orders in favour of the [EU] order of its rights and obligations arising from the Treaty, carries with it a clear limitation of their sovereign right upon which a subsequent unilateral law, incompatible with the aims of the [EU] cannot prevail. . . . It follows ... that the law stemming from the Treaty ... could not, because of its special and original nature, be over-ridden by domestic legal provisions, however framed, without being deprived of its character as [EU] law and without the legal basis of the [EU] itself being called into question.'

5.1.2

International Handelsgesellschaft GmbH v EVGF 11/70 [1970] ECR 1125

Key Facts

A German company challenged the legitimacy of an [EU] Regulation requiring export licences for agricultural products falling under the Common Agricultural Policy (CAP). Also payment of deposits was to be forfeited if no products were exported for the duration of the licence. The German court agreed that the measure was unconstitutional under German law as it infringed basic guaranteed rights to freely run a business and to be free of compulsory payment without proof of fault. In a reference to the ECJ the question was whether national constitutional law took precedence over [EU] law.

Key Law

The ECJ held that [EU] law takes precedence even over the constitutions of the Member States.

5.1.2

Simmenthal SpA v Amministrazione delle Finanze dello Stato 70/77 [1978] ECR 1453

Key Facts

An Italian firm imported beef from France and, under Italian law introduced in 1970, was bound to pay for inspection of the goods at the frontier. The Italian law was inconsistent with the requirements of Art 30 (now Art 34 TFEU) and [EU] Regulations of 1964 and 1968. The Italian court made an [Art 267 TFEU] reference to the ECJ on the question whether it must follow the [EU] law or wait for the Italian law to be annulled by the Italian constitutional court according to the usual procedure.

Key Law

The ECJ held that it must follow [EU] law in preference to any inconsistent national law.

Key Judgment

The court stated that 'directly applicable measures of the institutions . . . render automatically inapplicable any conflicting provision of current national law . . . and . . . also preclude the valid adoption of new national legislative measures to the extent that they would be incompatible with [EU] provisions. . .' As a result 'every national court must . . . apply [EU] law in its entirety and protect rights which the latter confers on individuals and must accordingly set aside any provision of national law which may conflict with it, whether prior or subsequent to the [EU] rule'.

5.1.3

R v Secretary of State for Transport ex p Factortame Ltd C-213/89 [1990] ECR I-2433

Key Facts

Companies registered in the UK but mostly owned by Spanish nationals were registered in the UK specifically to purchase trawlers registered in the UK. Under the Merchant Shipping Act 1988 and the Merchant Shipping (Registration of Fishing Vessels) Regulations 1988 there was a nationality requirement so that for registration a certain percentage ownership had to be in the hands of UK nationals. The applicants argued in the English court that the requirement was in breach of [Art 18 TFEU] in that it discriminated on nationality, as a result of which they were denied fishing rights otherwise guaranteed by [EU] law.

Key Law

The House of Lords (now the Supreme Court) had to decide whether to grant an interim injunction against an Act of Parliament, enacted after membership, which specifically contradicted [EU] law. The effect would be to suspend operation of the Act until the inconsistency issue could be settled on reference to the ECJ. As the House identified in its judgment, there was no rule in English constitutional law that would allow the injunction, nor could it see an overriding principle in [EU] law allowing a national court to suspend operation of a national law. In its reference the question was whether, in order to protect [EU] rights, a national court must grant the interim suspension of an Act of Parliament. The ECJ held that, to give effect to [EU] law, it must.

Key Judgment

The ECJ stated: 'It is for the national courts in application of the principle of co-operation laid down in [Art 4(3) TEU] . . . to set aside national legislative provisions which might prevent, even temporarily, [EU] rules from having full force and effect' and concluded that 'the full effectiveness of [EU] law would be just as much impaired if a rule of national law could prevent a court seized of a dispute governed by [EU] law from granting interim relief . . . It therefore follows that a court which in those circumstances would grant interim relief, if it were not for a rule of national law, is obliged to set aside that law.'

Key Comment

The case represents the most far-reaching statement of supremacy of EU law over national law and also demonstrates quite dramatically the supranational power of the institutions of the EU.

Key Link

Macarthys Ltd v Smith [1979] 1 WLR 1189: contrast with the early view on membership of Lord Denning: 'If the time should ever come when our Parliament deliberately passes an Act with the intention of repudiating the Treaty or any provisions in it, or intentionally of acting inconsistently with it, and says so in express terms, then I should have thought that it would be the duty of our courts to follow the statute of our Parliament.'

5.2.2

Van Gend en Loos v Nederlandse Administratie der Belastingen 26/62 [1963] ECR 1

Key Facts

The Dutch Government reclassified import duties, increasing duty on a chemical imported from Germany and causing increased cost to a Dutch bulb grower who argued that this breached [Art 30 TFEU]. The Dutch Government challenged the right of a citizen to invoke rights granted under the treaties and in the reference the question was whether a Treaty Article could create rights which nationals could enforce in national courts.

Key Law

The Advocate-General's reasoned decision suggested that, since the Article contained no explicit mention of individual rights, it could not be construed as granting individual rights and that, if the reclassification of the duty was contrary to [EU] law, the appropriate action should be by [Art 258 TFEU] proceedings. The ECJ, however, held that, since the Treaty was clearly intended to affect individuals, although [Art 30 TFEU] did not mention rights, it must clearly be capable of creating rights enforceable by individuals in national courts.

Key Judgment

The ECJ stated: 'Independently of the legislation of the Member States [EU] law . . . not only imposes obligations on individuals but is also intended to confer upon them rights which become part of their legal heritage . . . not only where they are expressly granted by the Treaty, but also by reason of obligations which the Treaty imposes in a clearly defined way upon individuals . . . Member States and the institutions of the [EU].' It added that [Art 30 TFEU] 'contains a clear and unconditional prohibition . . . ideally adapted to produce direct effects between member states and their subjects'. On [Art 258 TFEU] proceedings it stated: 'The fact that under this Article it is the Member States who are made the subject of the negative obligation does not imply that their nationals cannot benefit from this obligation. . . . The fact that the Article enables the Commission and the Member States to bring before the Court a State which has not fulfilled its obligations does not mean that individuals cannot plead these obligations. [Such] a restriction . . . would remove all direct legal protection of the individual rights of their nationals.'

5.2.5 *Leonesio v Ministero dell'Agricoltora & delle Foreste* 93/71 [1972] ECR 287

Key Facts

A Regulation introduced subsidies for dairy farmers prepared to slaughter their dairy herds in order to reduce the 'milk lake' (over-production of milk within the [EU]). The applicant had killed her cows but was then refused the subsidies by the Italian state.

Key Law

The ECJ held that the Regulation met the *Van Gend en Loos* (1963) criteria for direct effect. It was clear and precisely stated and was directly effective and enforceable by the applicant.

5.2.6 *Grad v Finanzamt Traustein* 9/70 [1970] ECR 825

Key Facts

A German company challenged a tax imposed on it, arguing that the tax breached a Directive requiring amendment to national VAT laws and also a Decision which gave a time limit for doing so.

Key Law

The ECJ decided that the company was entitled to rely on the decision provided that it satisfied the *Van Gend en Loos* criteria.

Key Judgment

The ECJ said it would be 'incompatible with the binding nature of decisions . . . to exclude the possibility that persons affected may [enforce them] . . . the effectiveness of such a measure would be weakened if . . . nationals . . . could not . . . invoke it . . . and the national courts could not take it into consideration'.

Key Problem

Since decisions are binding only on the party to whom they are addressed the lack of direct applicability that occurs with Directives does not apply. However, some of the problems that occur with Directives in relation to private parties could still occur if the party is not one to whom the decision is addressed.

5.2.7

Pubblico Ministero v Ratti 148/78 [1979] ECR 1629

Key Facts

Ratti was charged under Italian law for failing to properly label dangerous chemicals which he manufactured. His defence relied on two Directives requiring less stringent labelling than under Italian law. The date for implementation for one had expired without implementation but the other was still within the period.

Key Law

The ECJ held that when the time limit for implementation of a Directive has passed a citizen is entitled to rely on the Directive, but where that time limit has not yet expired then the Directive cannot have direct effect. Ratti was entitled to rely on the first Directive but not the one for which the time for implementation had not yet expired.

5.2.7

Marshall v Southampton and South West Hampshire AHA (No 1) 152/84 [1986] QB 401

Key Facts

A woman being forced to retire by her employer complained that the different retirement ages for men and women in the UK amounted to discrimination under the 'equal access Directive' (now under Directive 2006/54).

Key Law

The ECJ confirmed that the UK law failed to fully implement the Directive and identified that the woman could only rely on the improperly implemented Directive against her employer because it was the health service, an organ of the state. The Court recognised that Directives are only capable of vertical direct effect.

Key Judgment

The ECJ stated: 'According to [Art 288 TFEU] ... the binding nature of a directive ... exists only in relation to "each Member State to which it is addressed". It follows that a directive may not of itself impose obligations on an individual and that a provision of a directive may not be relied upon as such against such a person.'

5.2.7   *Duke v GEC Reliance Ltd* [1988] AC 618

Key Facts

On the same point as *Marshall* (1986), a woman did not wish to retire at the required age under UK law. Here, however, the woman was employed by a private company, not by the state.

Key Law

The House of Lords held that it was not bound to apply the equal treatment Directive because the Directive could not be effective horizontally. Even though the UK was at fault for failing to fully implement the Directive, the availability of a remedy then was entirely dependent on the identity of the employer. The House also rejected a request to apply the principle of indirect effect from *Von Colson* (1984).

Key Problem

The case shows that the availability of a remedy for a right given in a Directive is dependent on the nature of the party against whom the action is being brought. So it results in arbitrary justice.

5.2.7

Foster v British Gas plc C-188/89 [1990] ECR I-3313

Key Facts

The claimant argued that British Gas had breached the equal treatment Directive by making her retire at 60 when male employees retired at 65 (legitimate under s 6(4) Sex Discrimination Act 1975, later repealed in the Sex Discrimination Act 1986). At the time of her action British Gas was not a private company but was still owned by the state.

Key Law

The House of Lords (now the Supreme Court), in an [Art 267 TFEU] reference to the ECJ, asked the question whether British Gas was a body against which the Directive could be enforced. The ECJ identified that the national courts should decide what bodies a Directive could be enforced against using vertical direct effect. It also explained that vertical direct effect can apply not only to the state itself but also to bodies that could be described as an 'emanation of the state' (or 'arm of the state') which were ones that:

- provide a public service;
- are under the control of the state;
- have powers over and above those enjoyed by private bodies.

The House of Lords determined that, at the material time (before it was privatised), British Gas was an emanation of the state.

5.2.8

Von Colson and Kamann v Land Nordrhein-Westfalen 14/83 [1984] ECR 1891

Key Facts

Joined [Art 267 TFEU] references involved improper implementation of the equal treatment Directive by the German Government, a failure also seen in the second *Marshall* case (*Marshall v Southampton and South West Hampshire AHA (No 2)* C-271/91 [1993] 3 CMLR 293) provision of inadequate compensation under national law by contrast to full compensation required by the Directive. Von Colson applied to work for a state body, the prison service, while

Harz applied to work for a private company. Both were discriminated against contrary to the Directive.

Key Law

The ECJ held that the failure of German law to provide appropriate levels of compensation amounted to incomplete implementation of the Directive. However, while a remedy would have been available to Von Colson through vertical direct effect because the employer in question was the state, Harz would have been denied a remedy because of the anomaly resulting from lack of horizontal effect. The ECJ took a novel approach in resolving this problem. It employed the obligation in [Art 4(3) TEU] requiring Member States to give full effect to [EU] law and introduced the principle of 'indirect effect'. The German Court was bound to give full effect to the Directive and so must order full compensation in both cases.

Key Judgment

The court stated: 'Since the duty under [Art 4(3) TFEU] to ensure fulfilment of [an] obligation was binding on all national courts . . . it follows that . . . courts are required to interpret their national law in the light of the wording and purpose of the Directive.'

Key Comment

The ECJ ignored the problems created by the absence of horizontal direct effect of Directives. It created instead a means of overcoming those problems. Nevertheless, the judgment did leave ambiguous the question of to which national law the process of indirect effect could actually apply. This then allowed the House of Lords (now the Supreme Court) to refuse to apply the principle in *Duke* (1988), even though it would have been a means of providing a remedy for the applicant.

5.2.8 *Marleasing SA v La Commercial Internacional de Alimentacion SA* C-106/89 [1990] ECR I-4135

Key Facts

A company argued that another company was void for lack of cause under the Spanish Civil Code. The other company sought to rely on Directive 68/151 (on company law harmonisation), which listed all the grounds for invalidating companies but did not include that ground. Spain had not implemented the Directive at all, in contrast to *Von Colson* (1984) where the Directive was improperly implemented.

Key Law

In its reference the Spanish court asked the question whether the applicant could rely on the rules on the constitution of companies in Directive 68/151 since Spanish law conflicted with the provisions of the Directive. The ECJ applied the principles of indirect effect, held that the Spanish court was bound to give effect to the Directive and also expanded on the definition given in *Von Colson*.

Key Judgment

The ECJ explained that, 'in applying national law, whether the provisions concerned pre-date or post-date the Directive, the national court asked to interpret national law is bound to do so in every way possible in the light of the text and the aims of the Directive to achieve the results envisaged by it'.

Key Comment

Marleasing (1990) increases the scope of indirect effect significantly and has the effect of introducing horizontal direct effect by an indirect means, hence the title given to the process.

5.2.9   *Francovich and Bonifaci v Republic of Italy* C-6 and 9/90 [1991] ECR I-5357

Key Facts

Italy failed to introduce a scheme to provide a set minimum compensation for workers on insolvency of their employers. This breached a requirement under Directive 80/987. As a result of the failure to properly implement the Directive the claimants who had been made unemployed could not recover the wages due to them.

Key Law

The ECJ held that Italy was in breach of its obligations and, since there was no other remedy available to the claimants, the state was liable to compensate them for the loss resulting from its failure to implement the Directive. The Court introduced the principle that citizens can sue the state for non-implementation of a Directive.

It also confirmed that liability was not unlimited so that three conditions must be met:

● the Directive must confer rights on individuals;

● the contents of those rights must be identifiable in the wording of the measure;

● there must be a causal link between the damage suffered and the failure to implement the Directive.

The ECJ left a number of questions unanswered and left the issue of determining the extent of liability to the national courts.

Key Judgment

The ECJ stated that 'the full effectiveness of [EU] rules would be impaired and the rights they recognise would be undermined if individuals were unable to recover damages where their rights were infringed by a breach of [EU] law attributable to a member state'.

5.2.9

Brasserie du Pecheur SA v Federal Republic of Germany; R v Secretary of State for Transport, ex p Factortame Ltd (No 2) C-46 and 48/93 [1996] ECR I-1029

Key Facts

In joined references, one involved a German beer purity law challenged on the basis that it was in breach of [Art 34 TFEU], which prohibits quantitative restrictions on imports or exports or measures having an equivalent effect. The other involved quotas under the Merchant Shipping Act 1988, challenged as breaching [Art 49 TFEU], rights of establishment. It also involved a breach of a previous ECJ ruling. The reference was to clarify the conditions for state liability.

Key Law

The ECJ held that it was irrelevant that the breaches involved directly effective Treaty Articles and it was also irrelevant which organ of the Member State was in fact responsible for the breach. The court also redefined the conditions from *Francovich* to:

- the rule of [EU] law infringed must be intended to confer rights on individuals;
- the breach must be sufficiently serious to justify liability;
- there must be a direct causal link between the breach of the obligation imposed on the state and the damage actually suffered by the applicant.

Key Comment

The case widens the definition of the state to include acts and omissions of any organ of the state. The scope of liability is also extended beyond directives to include any breach of [EU] law, regardless of whether or not it has direct effect.

Key Link

See also *Kobler* C-224/01, where the principle of state liability was extended to courts of first instance, and *Traghetti del Mediterraneo SpA v Italy* C-173/03, where the Court of Justice held that 'the limitation on state liability solely to causes of intentional fault and serious misconduct on the part of the court [of last instance] is contrary to EU Law'.

5.2.9   *R v HM Treasury, ex p British Telecommunications plc* C-392/93 [1996] ECR I-1631

Key Facts

BT claimed that the UK Government had incorrectly implemented a Directive on public procurement in water, transport, energy and telecommunications as a result of which it suffered loss.

Key Law

The ECJ agreed that the Directive was imprecisely worded so that the meaning given to it by the UK Government was in fact possible. The court also accepted that the interpretation of the Directive was shared by other Member States. There was also no ECJ case law on the Directive to direct the Member State. Because of this the Court held that the breach was not 'sufficiently serious' to justify liability, as required by the *Brasserie du Pecheur* (1996) test.

Key Link

R v Ministry of Agriculture, Fisheries and Food, ex p Hedley Lomas (Ireland) Ltd C-5/94 [1996] ECR I-2553.

5.2.9 *Dillenkofer and others v Federal Republic of Germany* C-178,179, 188, 189 and 190/94 [1996] ECR I-4845

Key Facts

German law was challenged for failing to properly implement the Package Holidays Directive 90/314.

Key Law

The ECJ held that failure to implement a Directive by the due date is in itself a sufficiently serious breach to justify state liability and that there are situations where the seriousness of the breach is obvious so that imposition of state liability is almost a form of strict liability.

Key Comment

State liability diminishes the need to show direct effect or the rather strained construction of national law through indirect effect. Instead it focuses on the duty of the Member State to implement EU law and attaches rigorous sanctions for failure to implement so ultimately removes any possible advantage gained by non-implementation.

5.2 *Unilever Italia SpA v Central Food SpA* C-443/98 [2000] ECR I-7535

Key Facts

In a conflict over different labelling requirements the question was whether Directive 83/189 or Italian law should apply. Italy had introduced labelling requirements for the geographical origin of olive oil. Under the Directive Italy should have notified the Commission of its intention to regulate. The Commission intended to regulate itself [EU] wide, so under the Directive Italy should not have introduced the law. Unilever supplied Central Food without the labelling required by the Italian law and then refused to pay as the labelling did not conform to Italian law. It argued that the Italian law could not apply as this would breach the Directive.

Key Law

The ECJ held that the Italian law could not apply and that this did not conflict with the rules on horizontal direct effect of Directives since the Directive in this case did not involve rights on which individuals might rely. In other words the Court gave the Directive incidental horizontal effect.

Key Link

CIA Security International SA v Signalson and Securitel C-194/94 [1996] ECR I-2201, where there was no EC (now EU) right being relied on, and the Directive was merely being used to disapply national law.

5.3.3   *Broekmeulen v Huisarts Registratie Commissie* 246/80 [1981] ECR 2311

Key Facts

A doctor appealed to the Appeals Committee of the Royal Netherlands Society for the Protection of Medicine against a decision not to register him as a GP. His appeal was based on principles of [EU] Law and one issue for the ECJ was whether the appeals committee was a 'court or tribunal' for admissibility under the [Art 267 TFEU] reference procedure. Early case law of the ECJ had laid down five criteria: statutory origin, permanence, *inter partes* procedure, compulsory jurisdiction and the application of rules of law, and subsequent case law had also added independence.

Key Law

Taking a functionalist rather than a literalist approach, the ECJ held that the committee was a court for the purposes of [Art 267 TFEU].

Key Judgment

The ECJ stated that 'in the practical absence of redress before the ordinary courts . . . the appeal committee which performs its duties with the approval of the public authorities and operates with their assistance, and whose decisions are accepted following contentious proceedings and are in fact recognised as final, must be deemed to be a court'.

Key Link

Dorsch Consult C-54/96 [1997] ECR I-4961, which defined and followed the functional test meaning that more bodies can seek preliminary rulings than if a literalist test was applied.

Also *de Coster v Collège des bourgmestre et échevins de Watermael-Boitsfort* C-17/00 [2001] ECR I-9445. in which the Advocate-General described the approach of the ECJ as confused.

5.3.6 **_Foglia v Novello (No 2)_ 244/80 [1981] ECR 3045**

Key Facts

A French national ordered a consignment of Italian liqueur wine from an Italian wine merchant, Foglia, under a contract that stipulated that she should not be liable for any charges imposed by either French or Italian authorities, which would have been unlawful under [EU] law. The French customs did in fact impose a tax on the import which she paid and then tried to recover from the wine merchant. The Italian judge made a reference to the ECJ on the correct interpretation of [Art 110 TFEU].

Key Law

The ECJ refused the request for a preliminary ruling on the ground that it believed that the proceedings had been initiated by the parties purely to test the validity of French tax rules.

Key Comment

While the decision has been criticised there is no doubt that the reference did not in fact concern an issue of EU law and therefore the reference was inappropriate.

5.3.6

R (on the application of British American Tobacco) v Secretary of State for Health C-491/01 [2003] All ER (EC) 604

Key Facts

Here BAT and Imperial Tobacco were seeking a judicial review of UK legislation which was being used to implement Directive 2001/37 into English law. The Directive concerned regulation of maximum levels of tar, nicotine and carbon monoxide in cigarettes and also health warnings and other information to be provided on individual packets of cigarettes. The basis of the application for review was, among other things, that there was an inappropriate legislative basis for the introduction of the Directive. The Directive had been adopted under Art 95 and Art 133.

Key Law

In the reference to the ECJ, the Court held that the Directive was validly introduced under Art 95. Article 133 should not have been used but this did not affect the validity of the Directive.

5.3.4

CILFIT Srl v Ministero della Sanita 283/81 [1982] ECR 3415

Key Facts

Italian wool importers challenged a rule imposing a fee for an inspection of wool imported from outside the [EU] as contrary to Regulation 827/68. The argument was based on a provision in the Regulation, concerning the common organisation of the market in products listed in Annex II of the Treaty prohibiting any charges equivalent to a customs duty on imported animal products not specified or included elsewhere. The Italian Ministry of Health argued that as wool was not included in Annex II the Regulation could not apply and that the measure was so obvious as to remove any possible doubt requiring interpretation. A reference to the ECJ was made on the interpretation of paragraph 3 of [Art 267 TFEU], and whether the mandatory reference procedure required that a court of last resort has an absolute obligation to refer or whether it must only make a reference if it feels there is interpretative doubt.

Key Law

The ECJ held that a court or tribunal against whose decisions there is no judicial remedy under national law must refer unless it has established that the question before it is irrelevant, or there is a prior interpretation, or where the correct application of [EU] law is so obvious that it leaves no scope for reasonable doubt.

Key Judgment

The Court explained that it would not be necessary to refer 'if the answer to that question is not relevant, that is to say, if the answer to that question, regardless of what it might be, can in no way affect the outcome of the case' or where 'the authority of an interpretation ... already given by the Court may deprive the obligation of its purpose and thus empty it of its substance. Such [as] when the question is materially identical with a question which has already been the subject of a preliminary ruling in a similar case' or where 'the correct application of [EU] law may be so obvious as to leave no scope for reasonable doubt as to the manner in which the question raised is to be resolved. Before it comes to [that] conclusion the national court or tribunal must be convinced that the matter is equally obvious to the Courts of the other Member States and to the Court of Justice'.

Key Problem

The case has been the subject of a lot of criticism, particularly as it leaves too much discretion to the national courts, and it has been said that the criteria are too easy to manipulate by the national courts and thus it encourages them to decide too many difficult questions themselves, so jeopardising the uniform application of the Treaties. On the other hand it is also subject to calls for reform, particularly because of the delays caused by the backlog of cases. It is common for replies to referrals to take up to two years and in some cases there have been four-year waits.

6 Introduction to the law of the internal market

▶ 6.1 The aims of the single market

1   The internal market is a system of regional economic and social integration – a large trading unit in which there are no internal barriers to trade.

2   The internal market also aims towards monetary unity and political integration that will secure not only the economic welfare of the citizens of European states, but will also secure peace.

3   Since enlargement in 2004, the EU (by population) is the largest single trading bloc in the world. In 2013 it increased to 28 states, there are five countries with candidate status and three more that are potential applicants – so it will get much bigger.

▶ 6.2 The four freedoms

1   The logic of the founding Treaties was to create a single market, removing trade barriers based on national discrimination.

2   Hence the four freedoms identified in Art 26:

- free movement of workers;
- freedom to provide services;
- free movement of capital;
- free movement of goods.

3   Social mobility is ensured through Art 45 for workers, Art 49 for businesses or professions and Art 56 for providing services.

4   The purpose is to ensure that Member States do nothing to unfairly favour national enterprises and discriminate against enterprises from other Member States.

5   Free movement of goods is achieved in numerous ways:

● by prohibiting customs duties on imports and exports, and all other charges having equivalent effect (Art 30);

● by prohibiting discriminatory taxation (Art 110);

● by prohibiting quantitative restrictions (quotas) on imports and measures having equivalent effect (Art 34) and on exports (Art 35); exemptions exist in Art 36.

6   A Common Customs Tariff in Art 28 is governed by Art 31 and Art 32.

7   Goods are not defined in the Treaty, but have been defined as 'anything capable of money valuation and of being the object of commercial transactions . . .' (*Commission v Italy Re Export Tax on Art Treasures* 7/68).

8   Economic Monetary Union (EMU) is also a necessary development towards creating a truly internal market:

● so 17 members of the EU have moved towards a single currency;

● but problematic because of relative economic stability of different states;

● so 'convergence criteria' created;

● unfortunately the global recession caused by the banking crisis as well as economic problems specific to certain Member States including Greece, Italy Spain, Portugal and Ireland have led to a 'Eurozone' crisis also which is likely to lead to greater fiscal union between the Eurozone states – and in fact shows up that economic union really needs to be backed up by political union.

7 Art 34 and Art 35 and the free movement of goods

Prohibitions on quantitative restrictions – Art 34 and imports:

- Not defined in Treaty but is in case law – measures that amount to a total or partial restraint on imports, exports or goods in transit.
- So could include quota (*Salgoil SpA v Italian Minister of Trade*) or a complete ban on imports (*R v Henn & Darby*).
- Prohibited by Art 34.

Art 35 and exports:

- ECJ takes a different approach.
- Art 35 only restricts measures meant to differentiate between domestic and export trade and help exports at expense of other states (*Groenveld BV v Produktschap voor Vee en Vlees*).

Measures having equivalent effect (MEQRs):

- Not defined in Treaty, but in *Procureur du Roi v Dassonville* – all trading rules enacted by Member States which are capable of hindering, directly or indirectly, actually or potentially, intra-Community trade are to be considered as measures having an effect equivalent to quantitative restrictions – and are prohibited.
- But must distinguish between distinctly applicable (affects only imports) and indistinctly applicable (applies to imports and domestic goods – but affects imports disproportionately).
- But does not apply to selling arrangements if equally applied to imports and domestic goods (*Keck and Mithouard*).

FREE MOVEMENT OF GOODS

Cassis de Dijon principle:

- Principle in (*Cassis de Dijon case*) *Rewe-Zentral AG v Bundesmono-polverwaltung fur Branntwein*.
- Only applies to indistinctly applicable measures.
- Restriction lawful if to satisfy mandatory requirements for effective tax, protection of public health, fairness of commercial transactions or consumer protection – and proportionate.
- Second test – if product lawfully produced and marketed in one Member State then should be able to circulate freely throughout Community.

Art 36 derogations:

- Exemptions possible for public morality, public policy, or public security; protection of health of humans, animals or plants; protection of industrial and commercial property.
- List is exhaustive and narrower than *Cassis*.
- Art 36 can only be used if the measure is proportionate to the objective to be achieved, and non-arbitrary.
- Can only apply Art 36 to extent measure concerned is necessary to achieve objective – no further.
- Public morality varies by state (*R v Henn and Darby*).
- Public security only appropriate in crisis (*Campus Oil*).
- Public health must involve real risk to health (*Commission v UK (French Turkeys)*).

▶ 7.1 Prohibitions on quantitative restrictions on imports (Art 34) and exports (Art 35)

1   A quantitative restriction is a national measure that restricts the volume or amount of imports or exports, not by artificially raising the costs of importing or exports (as would be the case with a tariff or a tax), but by placing direct or indirect limits on the physical quantity of imports or exports that may enter or leave the market.

2   The Treaty deals with quantitative restrictions in:

- Art 34 in the case of imports;
- Art 35 in the case of exports;
- Art 36, which provides exemptions from the prohibitions if certain justifications are shown.

3   Quantitative restrictions are not defined in the Treaty:

- but they are in the case law: 'measures which amount to a total or partial restraint on imports, exports or goods in transit . . .' (*Geddo v Ente Nazionale Rist* 2/73);
- usually involves acts but can also be an omission (*Schmidberger v Austria* C-112/00);
- the most common form of QR is quotas (*Salgoil SpA v Italian Minister of Trade* 13/68);
- but can also include outright bans, e.g. a ban on importing porno-graphic material (*R v Henn & Darby* 34/79). And the Court of Justice has held that it also includes where a private individual is prohibited from importing alcoholic beverages (*Klas Rosengren and Others v Riksaklagaren* C-170/04).

▶ 7.2 Prohibitions on measures having equivalent effect (MEQRs)

1   'Measures having equivalent effect to a quantitative restriction' (MEQRs) are not defined in the Treaty, but have been widely inter-preted (*Commission v Ireland (Re discriminatory promotional policies)* 249/81).

2   Directive 70/50 (subsequently repealed) identified MEQRs as:

- distinctly applicable measures – those that apply only to imported goods and which make importing goods more difficult than using domestic products;

- indistinctly applicable measures – those that are equally applicable to imported and domestic goods, which only contravene Art 34 if their restrictive effect exceeds the effect intrinsic to trade rules.

3   Practices identified under the Directive have included:

- measures designed to specify less favourable prices for imports than for domestic products;

- practices establishing minimum and maximum prices below or above which imports are prohibited or reduced;

- standards subjecting imports to conditions relating to shape, size, weight or composition which cause them to suffer in competition with domestic products;

- laws restricting marketing of imported products in the absence of an agent/representative in the importing state.

4   But the definition is in the *Dassonville* formula: 'All trading rules enacted by Member States which are capable of hindering, directly or indirectly, actually or potentially, intra-Community trade are to be considered as measures having an effect equivalent to quantitative restrictions ...' (*Procureur du Roi v Dassonville* 8/74).

5   Distinctly applicable MEQRs have included:

- promoting domestic products (*Commission v Ireland (Buy Irish)* 249/81);

- import licence requirements (*International Fruit* 51 and 54/71);

- hygiene inspection for imports only (*Commission v UK (Re UHT Milk)* 124/81);

- and might even include a failure to ban a demonstration that closed a major transit route for 30 hours (*Schmidberger* C-112/00).

6   Indistinctly applicable MEQRs have included:

- origin marking (*Commission v UK* 207/83), and *Dassonville* was similar in requiring a certificate of origin;

- packaging requirements (*Walter Rau v De Smedt* 261/81) (Belgian requirement for margarine to be in cube-shaped packages);

- controls on ingredients (*Cassis de Dijon* 120/78), and *Commission v Germany (the Beer Purity case)* 178/84).

▶ 7.3 Art 36 and the derogations from Art 34 and Art 35

1   Art 36 provides derogations where 'justified on grounds of public morality, public policy, or public security; the protection of health and

life of humans, animals or plants; the protection of national treasures possessing artistic, historic or archaeological value; or the protection of industrial and commercial property ... prohibitions and restrictions shall not, however, constitute a means of arbitrary discrimination or a disguised restriction on trade between Member States ...'

2   So four key points stand out:

- list is also exhaustive (and narrower than *Cassis*);

- as a result, Art 36 must be construed strictly and narrowly;

- Member States may claim exemptions under Art 36 only to the extent that the measure concerned is justified (necessary) to achieve the objective, and no further;

- Art 36 only applies to QRs and distinctly applicable MEQRs (which are both direct discrimination).

3   So inevitably situations arise where the ECJ will not apply Art 36 (*Commission v Ireland* 113/80).

4   The ECJ has struggled to produce a truly EU interpretation of public morality since moral perceptions vary from state to state (*R v Henn and Darby* 34/79).

5   Cases where public morality was used as an Art 36 derogation include *Conegate Ltd v Customs and Excise Commissioners* 121/85 and *Quietlynn v Southend BC* C-23/89, which show that there must be a genuine issue of morality which is applicable to domestic goods also.

6   On public policy too, the ECJ has interpreted strictly but without achieving a EU concept (*Commission v Germany* 12/74 *(the Sekt case)*), and the ground has only been successfully used once (*R v Thompson and Others* 7/78).

7   Public security is only likely to be successfully claimed in relation to a crisis (*Campus Oil* 72/83).

8   Protecting the health and life of humans, animals and plants is a straightforward public health exception:

- The range of measures where a breach of Art 34 may occur includes import bans, licensing systems, inspections (particularly cross-border), prior authorisations, etc., any of which might be considered to be MEQRs (*Commission v UK (UHT Milk)* 124/81).

- But a real risk to health must be involved (*Commission v UK (French Turkeys)* 40/82).

- Art 36 can apply only if the measures are proportionate to the objectives to be achieved and protection of health cannot be achieved by other measures (*Commission v France (Re Italian Table Wines)* 42/82, but see also *Officier Van Justitie v Sandoz BV* 174/82, where a prohibition on an additive was allowed because there was no general medical consensus). The ECJ in *Greenham and Abel* C-95/01 laid down guidelines on the use of the health derogation for food additives – a Member State need not wait for absolute proof of risk but must not base a decision on purely hypothetical grounds.

- The real problem is the subjective character of analysing the real reasons for the restriction (*R v Secretary of State for the Home Department, ex parte Evans Medical and Macfarlane Smith* C-324/93).

- Failure of other states to operate according to recommendations but complying with a directive will not allow a state to rely on Art 36 (*R v Minister of Agriculture Fisheries and Food, ex parte Compassion in World Farming Ltd* C-1/96).

9   Protection of national treasures is a very precise area of justification, not yet successfully argued (*Commission v Italy (Re Export Tax on Art Treasures)* 7/68).

10 Protection of industrial and commercial property is, in effect, the intellectual property law of the EU and a giant area in its own right but property rights are difficult to define even in relation to a patent (*Centrafarm v Winthrop BV* 15 and 16/74).

11 But Art 36 has been used as a defence against national regulatory rules (*Torfaen BC v B and Q plc* 145/88).

▶ 7.4 The *Cassis de Dijon* principle

1   The wide scope of *Dassonville* meant that much indistinctly applicable national consumer protection legislation could breach Art 34 but was incapable of justification unless the health exemption could be used and the ECJ interprets Art 36 strictly and narrowly.

2   As a result the ECJ created the *Cassis de Dijon* rule of reason to allow Member States to plead a non-exhaustive list of 'mandatory requirements' including '*the effectiveness of fiscal provision, the protection of public health, the fairness of consumer transactions, and the defence of the consumer*' as justifications for possible breaches (*Rewe-Zentral AG v Bundesmonopolverwaltung fur Branntwein* 120/78 (*Cassis de Dijon case*)).

3   *Cassis* only applies to indistinctly applicable MEQRs which on the face of it are not discriminatory but could include a disguised discrimination:

- so the rule of reason allows the court to determine which the measure is;

- and only applies where the measure is necessary (*Familapress C-368/95*) and proportionate (*Clinique Laboratories C-315/92*);

- unlike Art 36 the list of exemptions is not fixed so has expanded to include, e.g., consumer protection (*Commission v Germany 178/84*), the improvement of working conditions (*Oebel 155/80*), the protection of the environment (*Commission v Danmark 302/86 (the Danish Bottles case)* and *Commission v Austria C-320/03*), protection of human rights (*Schmidberger v Austria C-112/00*), and the protection of a national industry (*Cinethique 60 and 61/84*).

4   A second rule from *Cassis*, the rule of mutual recognition, was that if a product was lawfully produced and marketed in one Member State then it should be able to circulate freely throughout the EU (since clarified by the Commission), but this can be rebutted (*Commission v Germany 174/84 (German Beer Purity)*).

5   However, the ECJ has also recognised that Art 34 has been used too often in attempts only to subvert national law, which has no effect on imports (*Keck and Mithouard C-267/91 and 268/91* (joined cases), where the ECJ held that the *Cassis de Dijon* principle will not apply to selling arrangements that apply to all relevant traders in the Member State, and that apply to both imports and domestic goods in the same way).

6   Selling arrangements also do not breach Art 34 and have included:

- restrictions on opening hours, e.g. Sunday trading (*Punto Casa C-69 and 258/93*);

- sales through specific outlets (*Quietlynn v Southend BC C-23/89*);

- advertising restrictions (*Hunermund 362/88 and Leclerc C-412/93*);

- but *Keck* will not apply where the domestic and imported goods will be affected differently under the national measure (*Konsumentombudsmannen (KO) v Gourmet International Products AB (GIP) C-405/98*) or where a less restrictive measure could be used to achieve the objective (*Ker-Optika bt v ANTSZ Del-dunátúli Regionalis Intézete C-108/09*).

▶ 7.5 Art 35 and exports

1   The ECJ takes a different approach to exports and Art 35.

2   Originally, the *Dassonville* formula was assumed to apply.

3   But the ECJ has ruled that Art 35 only restricts measures that are designed to differentiate between the domestic and export trade of a Member State so as to confer a benefit on exports at the expense of other states (*Groenveld BV v Produktschap voor Vee en Vlees 15/79*).

4   So measures applying equally to domestic products for the national market and those for export do not offend Art 35 (*Oebel* 155/80).

5   However, direct discrimination involving distinctly applicable measures does (*Bouhelier* 53/76).

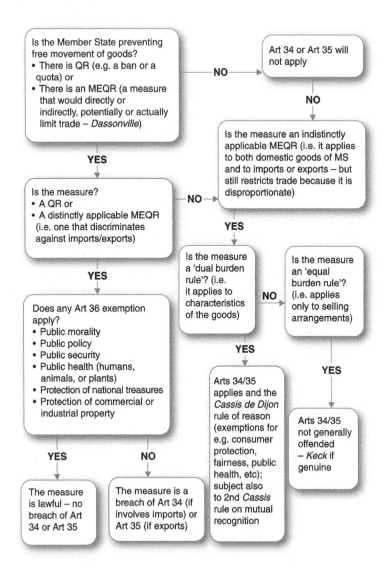

Flow chart illustrating the means of establishing breach of Art 34

Key Cases Checklist

QRs and distinctly applicable MEQRs

R v Henn & Darby (1979)
A QR is an outright ban on imports
Procureur du Roi v Dassonville (1974)
All rules capable of hindering directly, indirectly, actually or potentially trade between Member States are MEQRs
Commission v Ireland (The Buy Irish Campaign case) (1983)
A measure supported by the government designed to check the flow of inter-EU trade

Art 36 derogations

R v Henn and Darby (1979)
The definition of public morality varies from state to state
R v Thompson (1979)
Public policy can include trying to protect the right to mint coinage
Campus Oil (1984)
Public security only appropriate in crisis
Commission v UK (French Turkeys) (1982)
Public health must involve a real risk to health

Free Movement of Goods

Indistinctly applicable MEQRs and the 'rule of reason'

Rewe-Zentral AG v Bundesmonopolverwaltung fur Branntwein (Cassis de Dijon) (1979)
Developed the rule of reason – possible to exempt for reasons of health, consumer protection etc if necessary. Also the rule of 'mutual recognition' – if goods freely available in other Member States then no need to discriminate
Commission v Germany (The Beer Purity case) (1987)
But measure must be proportionate

Indistinctly applicable MEQRs and 'selling arrangements'

Keck and Mithouard (1993)
Application to products from other Member States of national provisions restricting or prohibiting certain selling arrangements does not hinder directly or indirectly, actually or potentially, trade between Member States – so no breach of Art 34, and *Cassis* does not apply
Vereinigte Familiapress Zeitungsverlags-und Vertreibs GmbH v Heinrich Bauer Verlag (1997)
Measures concerning something integral to the nature of the goods cannot be selling arrangements

7.1.3   *Klas Rosengren and Others v Riksaklagaren C-170/04*

Key Facts

Klas Rosengren and others ordered by correspondence a case of Spanish wine. Under Swedish law alcoholic beverages were only allowed to be imported by a body, Systembolaget, with a monopoly on such trade. The wine was confiscated by customs officers as a result and criminal proceedings brought against Rosengren and others. In a reference the question for the ECJ was whether this position was compatible with [Art 34 TFEU].

Key Law

The Court of Justice held that the fact that private individuals were prohibited from importing alcoholic beverages was a quantitative restriction contrary to [Art 34 TFEU].

7.2.1   *Commission v Ireland (The Buy Irish Campaign case)* 249/81 [1983] ECR 4005

Key Facts

Ireland wished to switch 3% of consumer trade away from imports to Irish products. The Government funded the Irish Goods Council which engaged in a 'Buy Irish' campaign. The Commission argued that this was a breach of [Art 34 TFEU].

Key Law

The ECJ held that the Irish Goods Council was an organ of the state and, while it had no power to introduce binding measures it was influential on Irish traders, so this amounted to a distinctly applicable MEQR and was a breach of [Art 34 TFEU].

Key Judgment

The court said it was 'a programme defined by the government which affects the national economy as a whole and which is intended to check the flow of trade between Member States'.

Key Comment

This shows how widely the ECJ views the responsibility of the state.

7.2.4   *Procureur du Roi v Dassonville* 8/74 [1974] ECR 837

Key Facts

A Belgian trader was prosecuted when he imported Scotch whisky from French suppliers without a certificate of origin as required by Belgian law. This was unavailable to him as it could only be issued by the UK customs authorities. He argued that the Belgian law was a breach of [Art 34 TFEU] and the ECJ agreed.

Key Law

The court held that the Belgian law indirectly discriminated against parties such as Dassonville, who did not import directly from Scotland but from France where the product was freely available.

Key Judgment

The court stated: 'All trading rules enacted by Member States which are capable of hindering, directly or indirectly, actually or potentially, intra-[EU] trade are to be considered as measures having an equivalent effect to quantitative restrictions.'

Key Comment

The case expanded on the definition provided by Directive 70/50 (since repealed), which identified two types of MEQR:

- distinctly applicable – measures applied only to imports but not to domestic products (direct discrimination);

- indistinctly applicable – measures applied to both but the effect on imports outweighs the general effect (not discriminatory on the face of it but could involve a disguised indirect discrimination).

Key Link

Geddo v Ente Nazionale Risi 2/73 [1973] ECR 865, which simply defines quantitative restrictions as 'measures which amount to a total or partial restraint on imports, exports or goods in transit'.

7.2.5

Commission v UK (The UHT Milk case) 124/81 [1983] ECR 203

Key Facts

The UK introduced an import licensing scheme. This also required re-treating and repackaging imported UHT milk.

The Commission challenged the measure as being in breach of [Art 34 TFEU]).

Key Law

The ECJ held that the licensing system was justified as it was necessary for regulating heat-treated milk and for tracing the origins of any infection. However, the other measures were unjustified since all Member States were subject to similar controls.

7.3.4   ### R v Henn and Darby 34/79 [1979] ECR 3795

Key Facts

English law prohibited importing of pornography. Henn and Darby were prosecuted, and argued that this breached [Art 34 TFEU].

Key Law

The ECJ held that the English law, in effect an outright ban, did amount to a quantitative restriction. However, the derogation of public morality under [Art 36 TFEU] was accepted as applying.

Key Judgment

The ECJ held: 'In principle, it is for each Member State to determine in accordance with its own scale of values and in the form selected by it the requirements of public morality in its territory.'

7.3.5   ### Conegate Ltd v Customs and Excise Commissioners 121/85 [1986] ECR 1007

Key Facts

A British company imported what were described as 'life-size inflatable rubber love dolls'. Customs officials seized a consignment of the dolls under s 42 Customs and Consolidation Act 1976 and relied on the public morality derogation under [Art 36 TFEU] in a claim that the seizure amounted to a breach of [Art 34 TFEU].

Key Law

The ECJ held that the derogation could not apply. The sale of such articles was not banned by the Act, although sale was restricted to licensed sex shops. The measure was being used as an arbitrary discrimination against imports and breached [Art 34 TFEU].

Key Link

R v Henn and Darby 34/79 [1979] ECR 3795 p 48.

7.3.6   ### *R v Thompson* 7/78 [1979] ECR 2247

Key Facts

English law prohibited the export of coins that were no longer legal tender. Thompson and two other men were convicted of breaching this law. They argued that the coins were goods since they were no longer legal tender, and that the law thus amounted to a breach of [Art 35 TFEU]. The UK sought to rely on the public policy exemption.

Key Law

The court held that the [Art 36 TFEU] exemption applied as the state was protecting coinage and preventing it from being melted down.

Key Judgment

The court stated: '[The] ban ... is justified ... because it stems from the need to protect the right to mint coinage which is traditionally regarded as involving the fundamental interests of the state.'

7.3.7   ### *Campus Oil Ltd* 72/83 [1984] ECR 2727

Key Facts

Irish law restricted imports of petrol, in effect meaning that petrol companies had to obtain 30% of their supplies from the only Irish oil refinery, located in Cork. In defence to a

claim that this was a breach of [Art 34 TFEU], the Irish
Government sought to rely on the public security defence
under [Art 36 TFEU], the argument being that over-reliance
on imports could threaten the security of the state at times
of shortage.

Key Law

The ECJ agreed that the defence could be appropriately
applied. Petrol was fundamental as an energy source and
essential not only to the public but to public services also.

Key Judgment

*The ECJ held that 'the aim of ensuring a minimum supply of
petroleum products at all times is to be regarded as tran-
scending purely economic considerations and thus capable
of constituting an objective covered by the concept of
public security'.*

7.3.8   *Commission v UK (The French Turkeys case)
40/82 [1982] ECR 2793*

Key Facts

A UK law banned the import of poultry. The UK Government
tried to justify the ban by arguing that it was to prevent
the spread of Newcastle Disease, a contagious condition
amongst poultry.

Key Law

The ECJ accepted that the ban was imposed in the run-up
to Christmas for purely economic reasons, particularly at
the expense of French imports. As such it was a quantitative restriction, in breach of [Art 34 TFEU], and the health
exemption could not apply.

Key Judgment

*The court held that 'The deduction must be made that
the ... measure did not form part of a seriously
considered health policy [and is] a disguised restriction on
imports'.*

7.3.8

Officiere van Justitite v Sandoz BV 174/82 [1983] ECR 2445

Key Facts

Dutch authorities refused to permit the sale of muesli bars with added vitamins and imposed a licensing requirement. Their argument was that excessive consumption of vitamins was harmful to public health. However, at the time there was no medical consensus on what amounted to excessive consumption.

Key Law

The ECJ held that, while the measure did appear to be a straightforward breach of [Art 34 TFEU], in the absence of Community harmonising measures identifying the sorts of additives that were harmful, Member States should decide the extent of the protection needed, subject to two requirements: that there should be no arbitrary discrimination and that the national measure must be proportionate to the actual risk.

7.3.8

Rewe-Zentralfinanz eGmbH v Landwirtschaftskammer 4/75 [1975] ECR 843

Key Facts

German law required all imported apples to be subject to phyto-sanitary inspection. It claimed the exemption, protection of health and life of humans, animals and plants, in [Art 36 TFEU] in that it was to protect against San Jose Scale, a disease prevalent in apples.

Key Law

The ECJ held that the defence could not be used since there was no similar inspection of domestically grown apples. The inspection made importing more difficult and more costly and was in effect a discrimination against imports and a breach of [Art 34 TFEU].

7.3.9   Commission v Italy (Re export tax on art treasures) 7/68 [1968] ECR 617

Key Facts

Italy imposed a tax on the export of anything of an artistic, historical or archaeological nature and argued that this was necessary to protect its art treasures, a vital part of its national heritage.

Key Law

The ECJ held that it was the effect of the discriminatory customs duties that was important, not its purpose. Here the effect was to hinder the export of any goods of the type identified and therefore it was a pecuniary burden and in breach.

Key Comment

The case actually concerned Art 30 TFEU (ex Art 12 EC Treaty) on tariffs but illustrates the exemption of protection of national treasures.

7.4.2   Rewe-Zentral AG v Bundesmonopolverwaltung fur Branntwein (The Cassis de Dijon case) 120/78 [1979] ECR 649

Key Facts

A German firm was prevented from importing a French blackcurrant liqueur, Cassis de Dijon. German law required such products to be a minimum alcoholic strength of 25% but the product was only 15%. The firm claimed the decision was a breach of [Art 34 TFEU]. Germany argued that the rule was necessary to protect public health in that by keeping alcohol strengths high it would discourage increases in alcohol consumption, also that it was fair to businesses which otherwise might be subject to a commercial disadvantage because the French product was inevitably cheaper.

Key Law

The ECJ laid down the 'rule of reason' that, in the case of indistinctly applicable MEQRs where a disguised discrimination was identified, Member States might justify this on grounds such as consumer protection, public health, fairness, etc. It also identified a second rule of 'mutual recognition', that once goods had been lawfully produced and sold in one Member State then they should be capable of import in all other Member States. The German rules were not necessary and were disproportionate since the same object could have been achieved by clear labelling.

Key Judgment

The Court said: 'Obstacles to [free] movement resulting from disparities between the national laws relating to the marketing of the products in question must be accepted in so far as these provisions are recognised as being necessary in order to satisfy mandatory requirements relating in particular to the effectiveness of fiscal supervision, the protection of public health, the fairness of commercial transactions and the defence of the consumer.'

Key Comment

The 'rule of reason' applies only to indistinctly applicable MEQRs to make up for the unfairness of Art 36 TFEU exemptions not being available. Unlike those exemptions the list is non-exhaustive.

7.4.3   *Clinique Laboratories and Estée Lauder Cosmetics* 315/92 [1994] ECR I-317

Key Facts

German law prohibited the sale of cosmetics under misleading names. German authorities prohibited Estée Lauder from marketing one of its cosmetics, Clinique, on the grounds that it could mislead consumers into believing that it had medicinal properties, thus causing the company excessive costs in repackaging.

Key Law

The ECJ held that there was a breach of [Art 34 TFEU] since the German law had a detrimental effect on imports and also was disproportionate to the objective. Estée Lauder's products were freely sold elsewhere without any confusion, and in any case in Germany they were only sold in cosmetics departments and never in pharmacies, so there was no consumer protection needed.

7.4.3

Cinetheque SA v Fédération Nationale des Cinémas Françaises 60 and 61/84 [1985] ECR 2605

Key Facts

French law prohibited sale or rental of films until one year after their release at the cinema. Cinetheque, a national video retail chain, challenged this law as being in breach of [Art 34 TFEU].

Key Law

The ECJ held that, while the law could hinder imports, it could also be justified for encouraging cinema attendance.

Key Judgment

The ECJ stated that 'a national system which, in order to encourage the creation of cinematographic works irrespective of their origin, gives priority, for a limited period, to the distribution of such works through the cinema is . . . justified'.

7.4.3

Schmidberger v Austria C-112/00 [2003] ECR I-5659

Key Facts

Austrian authorities allowed a road to be closed for the purposes of a demonstration by an environmental group. The decision was challenged by transport companies as a breach of [Art 34 TFEU] in that it restricted trade through preventing the transport of goods.

Key Law

The ECJ upheld the right of the Austrian authorities to use their discretion in such circumstances and held that to do otherwise would be to significantly undermine fundamental human rights, one aspect of which was the right to peaceful protest.

Key Comment

The case demonstrates a very significant application of the rule of reason and is clearly important in that fundamental human rights are a more basic right than free movement of goods.

7.4.4   *Commission v Germany (The Beer Purity case)* 178/84 [1987] ECR 1227

Key Facts

German law required that products could only be sold as 'bier' (beer) if made from malted barley, hops, yeast and water, although there was no restriction on marketing other products. The Commission alleged that this was a disguised discrimination against imports and a breach of [Art 34 TFEU]. Germany argued that it was necessary under the rule of reason for protection of consumers.

Key Law

The ECJ recognised the heavy beer consumption of German people and that some form of protection was appropriate. However, it held that the measure taken was disproportionate since the same objective could have been achieved through careful labelling.

7.3.11   *Torfaen Borough Council v B & Q plc* 145/88 [1989] ECR 3851

Key Facts

UK Sunday trading laws prohibited retail outlets from selling all but a small exempt range of products on Sundays. The law applied irrespective of the origin of the goods and was an 'equal burden' rule. The law led to numerous prosecutions and was challenged on the ground that it resulted in an estimated 10% reduction in trade.

Key Law

The ECJ held that the rule was justified on the basis that its sole purpose was to protect 'socio-cultural' characteristics. The only requirement was that the rule should be proportionate to the objective. This was for Member States to determine.

Key Problem

The case led to some inconsistent application by English courts. The socio-cultural characteristics included religious observance and also the protection of shop workers who did not wish to work on Sundays. English courts held this to be disproportionate since it could be secured by employment protection laws.

Key Link

B & Q plc v Shrewsbury Borough Council [1990] 3 CMLR 535; *Stoke-on-Trent City Council v B & Q plc* [1990] 3 CMLR 897.

7.4.5

Keck and Mithouard C-267 and 268/91 [1993] ECR I-6097

Key Facts

French law prohibited the re-sale of goods at lower than the purchase price, the justification being that it prevented large companies from undercutting smaller ones and putting them at a competitive disadvantage. Keck and Mithouard were prosecuted under the law and argued that the law breached [Art 34 TFEU].

Key Law

The ECJ identified the law as an 'equal burden' rule and introduced the concept of 'selling arrangements', which it held were not within the scope of [Art 34 TFEU] since they did not discriminate.

Key Judgment

The Court said: 'Such legislation may, admittedly, restrict the volume of sales . . . from other Member States, in so far as it deprives traders of a method of sales promotion. But the question remains whether such a possibility is sufficient to characterise the legislation in question as a measure having equivalent effect to a quantitative restriction on imports.' It added: 'Contrary to what has previously been decided, the application to products from other Member States of national provisions restricting or prohibiting certain selling arrangements is not such as to hinder directly or indirectly, actually or potentially, trade between Member States.'

Key Comment

Keck completes the cycle and means, together with the rule of reason, indistinctly applicable MEQRs can fall within Art 34 if they are a disguised restriction on trade, have exemptions through the rule of reason that are potentially broader than Art 36, and need not lead to unnecessary litigation where they have no effect on trade.

7.4.6

Vereinigte Familiapress Zeitungsverlags-und Vertreibs GmbH v Heinrich Bauer Verlag C-368/95 [1997] ECR I-3689

Key Facts

Austrian law prohibited the use of competitions for prizes in magazines. Familiapress tried to use this law in order to prevent a German magazine from publishing a magazine containing crossword puzzles for which prizes were available.

Key Law

The ECJ held that the puzzles were an integral part of the content of the goods and therefore could not fall within the rule on 'selling arrangements' in *Keck*, but instead should be given consideration under [Art 34 TFEU] to determine if they were a breach.

8

Art 30 and customs tariffs, and Art 110 and discriminatory taxation

ART 30 AND CUSTOMS DUTIES
ART 110 AND DISCRIMINATORY TAXATION

Art 30 and prohibitions on customs duties and measures having equivalent effect:

- Introduced to prevent Member States from subverting the single market by use of customs duties.
- Art 30 is directly effective (*Van Gend en Loos v Nederlandse Administratie der Belastingen*).
- The ECJ provides definition of MHEE – 'any pecuniary charge … imposed unilaterally on domestic or foreign goods [because] they cross a frontier and which is not a customs duty' (*Commission v Italy and Simmenthal v Italian Minister for Finance*).
- So, a disguised charge may be invalid (*Sociaal Fonds voor de Diamantarbeiders*).

Art 110 and prohibitions on discriminatory taxation:

- Two aspects to Art 110:
  - (i) no Member States should impose, directly or indirectly, on products of other Member States internal taxation in excess of that imposed on similar domestic products;
  - (ii) no Member States should impose an internal tax of such a nature to give protection to domestic products.
- To breach Art 110 the tax must discriminate against imports, e.g. applying sliding scales (*Humblot v Directeur des Services Fiscaux*) or only applying tax to imports (*Bobie v HZA Aachen-Nord*).

▶ 8.1 Art 30 and prohibition on customs duties and charges having equivalent effect

1   Customs duties are a very old device of protectionism.

2   So they were one of first mechanisms for the Treaty to attack.

3   To prevent Member States subverting the Treaties by introducing measures not called customs duties but with the same effect, the original EC Treaty prohibited any such measures.

4   All tariff barriers were removed in a transitional period following the EC Treaty.

5   Art 30 itself is a 'stand still' article prohibiting the introduction of any customs duties or provision having equivalent effect.

6   Art 30 is also directly effective, so as to be enforceable by citizens (*Van Gend en Loos v Nederlandse Administratie der Belastingen* 26/62).

7   Measures having equivalent effect are more problematic and not defined in the Treaty:

   ● so a definition is given by ECJ case law: 'any pecuniary charge . . . imposed unilaterally on domestic or foreign goods (because) they cross a frontier and which is not a customs duty in the strict sense constitutes a charge having equivalent effect . . . even if it is not imposed for the benefit of the state . . .' (*Commission v Italy* 24/68);

   ● reiterated in *Simmenthal v Italian Minister for Finance* 35/76 and *Bauhuis v Netherlands State* 46/76.

8   So a disguised charge may be an obstacle to trade and thus have equivalent effect and be invalid (*Sociaal Fonds voor de Diamantarbeiders* 2/69 and 3/69).

9   But a genuine tax will not, if within the requirements of Art 110.

10 A levy on services is permissible if:

   ● the cost is proportionate to the service received;

   ● it is in accordance with EU requirements;

   ● there is no discrimination between domestic and other EU goods (compare *Bauhuis v Netherlands* 46/76 with *Commission v Belgium* 132/82).

▌ 8.2 Art 110 and discriminatory taxation

1   Internal taxes may distort trade if differently applied:

- not preventing free movement but as a disincentive;
- more favourable tax regimes can have the same effect.

2   There are two aspects to Art 110:

- no Member States should impose, directly or indirectly, on the products of other Member States internal taxation in excess of that imposed on similar domestic products;
- no Member States should impose an internal tax of such a nature to give protection to domestic products.

3   But they should be construed as a whole, not separately (*Fazenda Publica v Americo* C-345/93).

4   Direct taxation is generally taken to refer to income tax, etc.:

- so Art 110 applies to indirect taxes;
- and means adopted to harmonise taxes include VAT.

5   'Internal taxation' is interpreted broadly, so might include:

- charges levied as a percentage of imported products, not general tax (*Iannelli v Meroni* 74/76);
- but can take account of, for example, higher cost of domestic raw materials (*Luxembourg v Belgium* 2/62 and 3/62);
- higher manufacturing costs (*Commission v Italy* 28/69).

6   Similar products are not defined in the Treaty but in case law:

- the ECJ tends to view similarity in terms of ways viewed by consumers rather than actual or potential use (*John Walker v Ministeriet for Skatter* 243/84);
- tax may be discriminatory if products are not so similar in character but do compete (*Commission v UK* 170/78).

7   Taxation must discriminate against imported products to offend Art 110:

- will do so particularly if sliding scales are applied (*Humblot v Directeur des Services Fiscaux* 112/84);
- and where imports but not domestic products are subject to fixed scales (*Bobie v HZA Aachen-Nord* 127/75).

Key Cases Checklist

> **Commission v Italy (Re Statistical Levy) (1969)**
> Any pecuniary charge imposed on imports or domestic goods because they
> cross a frontier equivalent to a customs duty and are unlawful

> **Arts 28–30 and Customs Tariffs**
> **Art 110 and Discriminatory Taxation**

> **Commission v France (Reprographic Machines) (1981)**
> A genuine tax is a system of internal duties applied systematically to
> categories of products in accordance with objective criteria irrespective of origin

8.1.7

Commission v Italy (Re Statistical Levy) 24/68 [1969] ECR 193

Key Facts

The Italian Government levied a charge on all imports and exports in order to fund a statistical service on trade patterns. This was challenged by the Commission as being a fiscal barrier to trade.

Key Law

The ECJ held that there was a breach of [Art 30 TFEU] and dismissed the argument that it was for the benefit of importers. Any advantage that they might gain was too uncertain and too general for the benefit to be measured. The Treaty called for the abolition of all import duties and any charges having an equivalent effect and the levy fell within that definition.

Key Judgment

The Court stated that 'any pecuniary charge ... which is imposed unilaterally on domestic or foreign goods by reason of the fact that they cross a frontier and which is not a customs duty in the strict sense constitutes a charge having equivalent effect within the meaning of ... the Treaty, even if it is not imposed for the benefit of the state, is not discriminatory or protective in effect'.

8.1.8

Sociaal Fonds voor de Diamantarbeiders v Chougol Diamond Co 2/69 and 3/69 [1969] ECR 211

Key Facts

Belgium imposed a duty on the import of uncut diamonds from South Africa. It was challenged as a breach of [Art 30 TFEU].

Key Law

The Court held that, even though the duty was not to protect the domestic market since there are no diamond mines in Belgium, nevertheless [Art 30 TFEU] applied because the duty was designed to make imports more expensive.

Kapniki Mikhailidis C-441 and 442/98 [2000] ECR I-7415

Key Facts

A duty was imposed on the export of tobacco products from Greece. The argument was that the charge was justified because it was to raise money for workers in the tobacco industry.

Key Law

The Court rejected the argument. There are no derogations, as there would be for [Art 34 TFEU] and [Art 35 TFEU]. The only justification is where the charge is payment for services of a tangible benefit to the importer or exporter. Even then the charge must not exceed the value of the service provided.

De Danske Bilimportorer C-383/01 [2003] ECR I-6065

Key Facts

A Danish company bought and imported a new car from Germany. Danish law required all new cars to be registered and payment of a registration charge, which in this case amounted to 40,000 euros. Since the car had only cost 27,000 euros the company claimed that there was a breach of [Art 110 TFEU].

Key Law

The Court held that there was no breach because Denmark did not make cars so there was no similar domestic product and [Art 110 TFEU] only applies if the tax is discriminatory or protects domestic goods.

Key Problem

[Article 110 TFEU] allows Member States a complete discretion on imposing taxes on goods that are non-discriminatory and not for protection of domestic goods and there can be no breach if the domestic product is then more expensive. This for example results in the high taxes on cigarettes, alcohol and petrol in the UK and has led to extra work for customs trying to control people who bring in unlimited amounts with a view to commercial gain.

Commission v France (Reprographic Machines) 90/79 [1981] ECR 283

Key Facts

A French charge on reprographic machines was challenged by the Commission. The question for the Court was whether it was a customs duty disguised as a tax breaching [Art 30 TFEU] or a genuine tax falling under [Art 110 TFEU], if discriminatory or protectionist.

Key Law

The Court held that a tax may be imposed on imported products if there is no competing domestic product as long as the tax applies to a class of product irrespective of its origin.

Key Judgment

The Court defined a genuine tax as 'a general system of internal duties applied systematically to categories of products in accordance with objective criteria irrespective of the origin of the products'.

Commission v Luxembourg (Re Import on Gingerbread) 2/62 and 3/62 [1962] ECR 425

Key Facts

Luxembourg imposed a compensatory tax on imported gingerbread which it argued was introduced merely to compensate for the competitive disadvantage which resulted from a high domestic tax on one of the ingredients.

Key Law

The Court held that this was in reality a customs duty disguised as a tax. Duties merely called compensatory taxes could not be allowed to stand. To do so would allow Member States to call anything a tax and justify it by calling it compensatory when the actual effect would be to prevent genuine competition from exports.

8.2.7

Humblot v Directeur des Services Fiscaux 112/84 [1987] ECR 1367

Key Facts

Humblot, a French national, bought and imported a Mercedes car from Germany. French road tax was charged on a sliding scale up to a certain engine capacity for which 1,000 francs was payable. For cars over this engine capacity, as the Mercedes was, there was a single charge of 5,000 francs. Humblot paid the tax but tried to reclaim it through the French courts. A reference was made.

Key Law

The ECJ held that the 5,000 franc charge was excessive and, although *prima facie* non-discriminatory as it applied to all cars, in fact had the effect of discriminating against imports since France did not at the time produce cars over the set engine capacity. There was a breach of [Art 110 TFEU].

Commission v France (Taxation of Spirits)
168/78 [1980] ECR 347

Key Facts

French law imposed significantly higher taxes on spirits distilled from cereals, such as whisky and gin, than it did on spirits distilled from fruits or grapes, such as cognac, armagnac and brandy. The first group were mostly imported and the second involved significant domestic production. As a result the Commission challenged the tax system as being contrary to [Art 110 TFEU]. The French Government argued that the products were very different, both in taste and in the way in which they would be drunk in France, i.e. the first would be diluted and often drunk as an aperitif, while the latter group would be drunk neat.

Key Law

The ECJ rejected the argument that there was a distinction between the grain-based and fruit-based drinks. It was not based on any objective justification since individuals might have widely differing drinking habits. The Court felt that it did not need to consider whether the drinks were in fact similar because it was a fact that they were in competition. [Art 110 TFEU] applied and there was a breach.

Key Judgment

The Court held that 'it is necessary to consider as "similar" products which have similar characteristics and meet the same needs [of] consumers. It is therefore necessary to determine the scope of [Art 110 TFEU] on the basis not of the criterion of the strictly identical nature of the products but on that of their similar and comparable use'.

Key Link

FG Roders BV C-367 to 377/93 [1995] ECR I-2229, which involved a thorough examination of the different qualities and similarities of a variety of alcoholic drinks.

9 Art 45 and the free movement of workers

Definition of worker:

- pursuit of effective and genuine activity (*Levin v Staatssecretaris van Justitie*);
- performs service in return for remuneration (*Lawrie-Blum v Land Baden-urttemberg*);
- worker who has lost job but is capable of finding other work (*Hoekstra*);
- part-timer needing supplementary benefit (*Kempf v Staatsecretaris voor Justitie*);
- no formal wage but involved in economic activity (*Steymann v Staatsecretaris voor Justitie*);
- person looking for work (*R v Immigration Appeal Tribunal, ex parte Antonissen*);
- but not if not for a genuine reason (*Bettray v Staatssecretaris van Justitie*);
- now Directive 2004/38 incorporates these definitions – (Art 7(3)) identifies situations in which worker status will not be lost:
- temporarily unable to work through sickness or accident;
- involuntary unemployment after one year's employment in host state and is registered job seeker;
- involuntary unemployment after fixed term contract of under a year;
- involuntary unemployment and embarks on vocational course.

Rights of entry and residence

- Directive 2004/38 Art 5(1) – can leave home state to seek employment in another state and enter on production of valid identity card or passport, and get residence permit with relevant documents;
- can enter and look for work (*Procureur du Roi v Royer*);
- for at least 6 months (*R v Immigration Appeal Tribunal ex parte Antonissen*);
- Directive 2004/38 Art 6 gives all EU citizens automatic right of residence in any Member State for three months.

Equal treatment:

Regulation 1612/68 demands equal treatment in all employment matters, including:

- no limiting offers of employment or number of migrant workers (*Commission v France (Re French Merchant Seamen)*);
- linguistic tests are valid (*Groener v Minister of Education*);
- equal conditions for nationals and migrants in pay, conditions, dismissals (*Wurttembergische Milchvertung-Sudmilch AG v Ugliola*);
- dependents have rights to live with worker irrespective of nationality (*Lebon*).

Definition of families:

- Directive 2004/38 Art 2(2) gives right to spouses, dependants under 21, ascendant relatives and registered partners;
- Directive 2004/38 Art 3(2) also gives rights to any actual family dependents and partners of the worker in a durable relationship;
- and cohabitees (*Netherlands State v Anne Florence Reed*) may be a social advantage to the worker.

Right to remain after employment:

- Directive 2004/38 gives right to remain after five years' continuous residence.

FREE MOVEMENT OF WORKERS

Limitations of free movement

- Art 45(3) and Directive 2004/38 Art 27(1) allow derogations for public policy, public security, public health.
- Public policy for genuine threat to society (*R v Bouchereau*).
- But not if not illegal in host state (*Adoui & Cornaille v Belgium*).
- Public policy or security must be exclusively on conduct of individual concerned (*Van Duyn v The Home Office*).
- Public health Directive 2004/38 Art 29(1) lists prescribed diseases, e.g. TB.
- Art 45(4) permits limiting access to public service on nationality.
- Applies only to civil authority or security of state (*Commission v Belgium*).

▶ 9.1 Introduction

1 This was essential to the creation of the internal market.

2 Art 45 requires free movement of workers within the EU.

3 The basis for free movement is in Art 18: 'any discrimination on grounds of nationality shall be prohibited . . .'

4 Found in Arts 45–48 and regulations and directives.

5 Equivalent rights exist in Art 49 and Art 56 for professionals and businesses.

▶ 9.2 The character and extent of Art 45

1 Member States are required to prohibit any discrimination between workers of different states based on nationality.

2 And to apply equality to employment, remuneration and all other conditions of employment, e.g. the same for migrant workers as for workers of the host nation.

3 A state can derogate on public security, public health or public policy grounds, and exclude from public service.

4 The extent of the right is:

● to take up offers of work already made;

● to move freely throughout EU to seek employment;

● to remain in a Member State for employment under the same conditions as a national of the Member State;

● to remain after employment.

▶ 9.3 The definition of 'worker'

1 Art 45 applies to 'workers', but no definition is provided.

2 So definition has come from numerous Art 267 references but is now also under Directive 2004/38.

3 'Citizenship' created in TEU is not the same as a 'worker'.

4 The earliest definition held Art 45 applied only to 'the pursuit of effective and genuine activities to the exclusion of activities of such a small scale as to be regarded as purely marginal and ancillary . . .' (*Levin v Staatssecretaris van Justitie* 53/81).

5   Essential characteristics of a worker are 'performance of services, under the direction of another, in return for remuneration, for a certain period of time . . .' (*Lawrie-Blum v Land Baden-Wurttemberg* 66/85).

6   The ECJ has interpreted the definition of 'worker ' liberally:

- a worker who has lost his job but is capable of finding other work (*Hoekstra v Bestuur der Badrijfsvereniging voor Detailhandel en Ambachten* 75/63) and *Leclere and Deaconescu* C-43/99;

- a part-timer needing supplementary benefit for subsistence (*Kempf v Staatssecretaris voor Justitie* 139/85);

- a person with no formal wage but involved in an economic activity (*Steymann v Staatssecretaris voor Justitie* 196/87; *Trojani* C-456/02;

- a professional sportsman (*Dona v Mantero* 13/76);

- a person looking for work (R *v Immigration Appeal Tribunal, ex parte Antonissen* 292/89).

7   However, the ECJ has also imposed limitations:

- where there is no economic purpose to the activity (*Bettray v Staatssecretaris van Justitie* 344/87);

- if the sport is not a genuine economic activity (*Walrave & Koch v Association Union Cycliste Internationale* 36/74).

8   Directive 2004/38 also identifies situations where worker status is not lost:

- a worker is temporarily unable to work through sickness or accident;

- involuntary unemployment after one year's employment in the host state and the worker is a registered job seeker;

- involuntary unemployment after a fixed term contract of under a year;

- involuntary unemployment and the worker takes a vocational course.

▶ 9.4 Workers' families

1   Art 45 gives rights to workers' families:

- Directive 2004/38 provides a new definition of family members in Art 2(2): a) a spouse; b) a registered partner (where the host state treats registered partners as equivalent to marriage); c) direct descendants under 21 who are dependents, and those of the partner; d) dependent direct ascending relatives;

- Art 3(2) also includes a) any other family members whether EU citizens or not who are dependents or require personal care of a worker; b) a partner with whom the EU citizen has a durable relationship, i.e. genuine cohabitees.

2   Sometimes rights extend to cohabitees (*Netherlands State v Anne Florence Reed 59/85*) if this ensures equal social and tax advantages to the worker.

3   Rights are not lost through mere separation (*Diatta v Land Berlin 267/83*).

4   But may be with complete marital breakdown (*R v Secretary of State for the Home Department, ex parte Sandhu* (1983)).

▶ 9.5 Rights of entry and residence

1   These rights are identified in Directive 2004/38 Art 5(1):

- to leave home state to seek employment in another state;
- to enter another state 'on production of a valid identity card or passport (or proof of relationship with the worker) . . .' (non-EU nationals need visas);
- to notify the relevant authorities.

2   By Directive 2004/38 Art 6 all EU citizens have right of residence in any other Member State for up to three months on production of a passport or identity card – non-EU family members accompanying the EU national have the same rights but require a visa. Under Directive 2004/38 Art 16(1) permanent right of residence is gained after five years' continuous residence; see *Tomasz Ziolkowski* C-424/10 and *Barbara Szeja, Maria-Magdalena Szeja, Marlon Szeja v Land Berlin* C-425/10.

3   The right includes to enter and look for work (*Proceurer de Roi v Royer 48/75*).

4   There is no fixed time limit, but six months has been held sufficient, justifying removal if passed (*R v Immigration Appeal Tribunal, ex parte Antonissen* C-292/89) (three months in *Royer*). Under Directive 2004/38 the worker is allowed to stay until he becomes an unreasonable burden on the state.

5   Failures to observe formalities do not justify refusal to allow entry or residence (*R v Pieck* 157/79).

6   Nor do they justify deportation (*Watson & Belmann* 118/75).

7   Seasonal workers are allowed temporary residence permits.

▶ 9.6 The right to equal treatment

1   Art 45 requires abolition of discrimination on nationality in employment, remuneration and conditions.

2   Regulation 1612/68 requires equal treatment in all employment matters and elimination of obstacles to mobility. It has three Titles:

- Title I – eligibility for employment:

  i) Art 3 prohibits limiting offers of employment or restricting numbers of migrant workers (*Commission v France (Re French Merchant Seamen)* 167/73);

  ii) Art 5 no discriminatory tests for recruitment, e.g. vocational, medical or other;

  iii) linguistic tests are valid (*Groener v Minister of Education* 378/87).

- Title II – equality in conditions of employment:

  i) Art 7(1) ensures equal conditions for nationals and migrants in pay, conditions, dismissals, etc. (*Wurttembergische Milchvertung-Sudmilch AG v Ugliola* 15/69; *Sotgiu v Deutsche Bundespost* 152/73, *Kobler* C-224/01 and *Merida* C-400/02);

  ii) by Art 7(2) migrants should receive the same tax and social advantages as nationals, which may survive the death of the worker (*Fiorini v SNCF* 32/75);

  iii) the right exists whether or not linked to a contract of employment (*Ministere Public v Even* 207/78);

  iv) social advantage can include, for example, a grant (*Brown* 197/86);

  v) access to social advantages is conditional on worker status – so to gain social security benefits, a work-seeker must be genuinely seeking work but a denial of those benefits must be objective and proportionate (*Collins* C-138/02 and *Ioannidis* C-258/04).

- Title III – workers' families.

    i) Art 10(1) gave family, if dependants, rights to live with worker irrespective of their nationality (*Lebon* 316/85); now Directive 2004/38 Art 14(1) guarantees the right but;

    ii) Art 11 gives the right to take employment regardless of nationality (*Gul* 131/85);

    iii) Art 12 gives workers' children the same rights as nationals to education, training and apprenticeship:

        a) so they can receive grants (*GBC Echtemach and A Moritz v Netherlands Minister for Education* 389/87 and 390/87);

        b) and may be exempt from fees if nationals are (*Forcheri v Belgian State* 152/82);

        c) ECJ takes a broad view of 'vocational training' which may include university degrees (*Gravier v Liege* 293/83 and *Blaizot v University of Liege* 24/86);

        d) and Art 12 rights continue even on death of worker (*Michel* 76/62 and *Casagrande* 9/74).

▶ 9.7 The right to permanent residence under Directive 2004/38

1   By Art 16(1) all EU citizens gain the right to permanent residence after a period of five years' continuous residence in the host state.

2   The same rule applies to non-EU family members who have lived in the host state continuously for five years with the citizen.

3   Under Art 16(3) continuous residence is not affected by:

    i) temporary absences under six months in a year;

    ii) absences for military service;

    iii) one absence for up to 12 months for e.g. pregnancy, illness, vocational training etc.

4   Under Art 17 permanent residence can also be gained under the five-year qualifying period if the EU citizen who is a worker or self-employed;

    i) has reached retirement age;

    ii) becomes permanently incapable of working;

    iii) lives in the host state but works in another state.

5   Also under Art 17 families of the EU citizen who is a worker or self-employed also gain permanent residence if the worker dies before the five years, provided that

   i) the worker/self-employed person had resided for two continuous years in the host state;

   ii) the death occurred because of accident at work or occupational disease;

   iii) the surviving spouse lost nationality of the state following marriage.

▶ 9.8 Free movement and professional sport

1   Sport, particularly football, raises problems under Art 45, i.e. transfer system, limitations on numbers of foreign players.

2   The ability of managers to move freely throughout the community has been established (*UNECTEF v Heylens* 222/86).

3   The ECJ in the *Bosman* ruling has major implications for football:

   ● Art 45 prohibits transfer fees once a contract has terminated;

   ● it restricts numbers (*Bosman* C-415/93).

4   A scheme to encourage restricting taking up contracts elsewhere after being a trainee footballer for one club in order to encourage the provision of training of young players does not breach Art 45 unless it is disproportionate and goes beyond what is necessary to achieve the objective (*Olympique Lyonnais SASP v Olivier Bernard and Newcastle United FC* C-325/08).

▶ 9.9 Social security provisions

1   Art 48 requires aggregation of all periods of work in the community for eligibility to benefits.

2   Implemented by Regulation 1408/71 – did not harmonise social security systems but required application of systems so as not to penalise a worker and prevent him using Art 45.

3   The key principles were:

   ● universality of eligibility and of benefits;

- non-discrimination (meaning migrant workers cannot be excluded from national systems);

- aggregated and not concurrent benefits.

4   In 2010 Regulation 883/2004 (as amended by Regulation 988/2009) replaced Regulation 1408/71:

- its scope is broader than the earlier Regulation as it applies not just to the employed/self-employed and their families, but others who are not economically active;

- it simplifies the procedure and aims to facilitate free movement of citizens irrespective of economic status.

▶ 9.10 Limitations on free movement

1   Contained in Art 45(3) – Member States can introduce rules which limit the exercise of free movement based 'on grounds of public policy, public security or public health . . .'

2   Directive 2004/38 Art 27(1) lays down principles on all three – extends to all EU nationals who reside in or travel in another Member State, as employees, self-employed, or as families.

3   Art 27(1) – derogation cannot be used for economic ends.

4   By Art 27(2), measures taken on public policy or public security:

- must be taken exclusively on the conduct of the individual concerned (*Van Duyn v The Home Office* 41/74);

- personal conduct is strictly interpreted (*Rutili v Ministère de l'Interieur* 36/75);

- and must comply with the principle of proportionality (*Watson and Belmann* 118/75);

- and a restriction on movement is permissible only if it is objectively justified (*Omega* C-36/02).

5   Public policy can only be invoked where there is a genuine present and sufficiently serious threat to the interests of society (*R v Bouchereau* 30/77). Also:

- past convictions alone are insufficient to invoke the exception: Art 27(2) (*Bonsignore v Oberstadtdirecktor of the City of Cologne* 67/74 and *Oliveri* C-493/01);

- exclusion cannot be for activity not illegal in the host state (*Adoui and Cornaille v Belgian State* 115/81 and 116/81);

- mere expiry of an ID card or passport is never sufficient ground for deportation (*Watson and Belmann* 118/75).

6   The difference between public policy and public security is vague.

7   Art 29 identifies prescribed diseases justifying refusal of entry:

- those with epidemic potential as defined by the relevant instruments of the World Health Organization;

- other infectious diseases or other contagious parasitic diseases if they are subject to protection provisions applying to nationals of the host state.

8   Procedural safeguards include:

- by Art 30(1) the decision to exclude/deport must be notified in writing in a manner that the recipient can understand;

- by Art 30(2) the grounds for the decision must be given in full;

- by Art 30(3) they must be notified of the appeals procedure;

- by Art 31 they have access to judicial and appropriate administrative redress which must determine that the decision is not disproportionate.

▶ 9.11 Public service employment

1   Art 45(4) allows Member States to deny/restrict access to workers in public service on the basis of their nationality.

2   But the ECJ has interpreted this provision fairly narrowly:

- it does not apply to all public service, only exercise of civil authority or security of state (*Commission v Belgium (Re Public Employees)* 149/79);

- it applies only to access to employment, not to conditions (*Sotgiu v Deutsche Bundespost* 152/73);

- so cannot reserve posts in hospitals for nationals (*Commission v France (Re French Nurses)* 307/84);

- or in teaching (*Bleis v Ministere de l'Education* C-4/91);

- or impose unnecessary qualifications on non-nationals (*Groener Minister for Education* 397/87).

Key Cases Checklist

Definition of worker

***Levin v Staatsecretaris van Justitie* (1982)**
Pursuit of effective & genuine economic activity
***Lawrie-Blum v Land Baden-Wurttemberg* (1986)**
Performs service, in return for remuneration
***Steymann v Staatssecretaris voor Justitie* (1988)**
No formal wage but involved in economic activity
***R v Immigration Appeal Tribunal ex parte Antonissen* (1991)**
Person looking for work but not if not for a genuine reason

Workers' families

***Netherlands State v Anne Florence Reed* (1986)**
A cohabitee is not a family member but it may infringe the worker's rights to deny him access
***Centre Public d'Aide Sociale Courcelles v Lebon* (1987)**
Who is a dependent is a question of fact for the court to decide

Free Movement of Workers

Limitations on free movement

***Van Duyn v The Home Office* (1974)**
Public policy or security must be exclusively on conduct of individual concerned
***R v Bouchereau* (1978)**
And must represent a current genuine threat to society
***Adoui & Cornaille v Belgium* (1982)**
Cannot use the exemption if the activity is not illegal in the host state
***Commission v Belgium* (1980)**
The public service exemption applies only to civil authority or security of state

Rights of entry and residence

***Procureur du Roi v Royer* (1976)**
Can look for work and rights of residence does not depend on permit

Equal treatment

***Commission v France (Re French Merchant Seamen)* (1974)**
There should be no limiting on offers of employment or numbers of migrant workers
***Groener v Minister for Education* (1989)**
Although linguistic tests are valid
***Wurttembergische Milchvertung-Sudmilch AG v Ugliola* (1969)**
There should be equal conditions for nationals & migrants in pay, conditions, and dismissals
***Fiorini v SNCF* (1975)**
And families of migrant workers should enjoy the same social rights as those of host state workers
***Casagrande v Landeshauptstadt Munchen* (1974)**
Including education

9.3.4   *Levin v Staatssecretaris van Justitie* 53/8 [1982] ECR 1035

Key Facts

A British woman and her South African husband moved to the Netherlands and were financially independent. The Dutch authorities were reluctant to allow them residence so she took part-time work for a low wage, under the Dutch minimum wage, so the Dutch authorities refused to recognise her as a worker.

Key Law

The ECJ would not accept that the term 'worker' could be defined quantitatively. Instead it should be measured qualitatively.

Key Judgment

The ECJ defined work as 'the pursuit of effective and genuine activities, to the exclusion of activities on such a small scale as to be regarded as marginal and ancillary'.

9.3.5   *Lawrie-Blum v Land Baden-Wurttemberg* 66/85 [1986] ECR 2121

Key Facts

A British national was refused entry onto a teacher training course in Germany on national grounds alone. Germany rejected her claim that this breached her [Art 45 TFEU] rights to free movement of workers.

Key Law

The ECJ held that she could be classed as a worker as she would receive a small salary as a trainee teacher and would be required to teach up to 11 hours per week. The level of pay and hours worked were not material in determining her status as a worker.

Key Judgment

The ECJ stated that 'The essential feature of an employment relationship is that for a certain period of time a person performs services for and under the direction of another in return for which he receives remuneration'.

9.3.6

Kempf v Staatssecretaris voor Justitie 139/85 [1986] ECR 1741

Key Facts

A German national worked for 12 hours per week in Holland teaching music. His pay was too low to live on so he claimed supplementary benefit. His application for a work permit was rejected because his income was too low to support him.

Key Law

The ECJ held that the mere fact that his income was so low that he required assistance did not prevent him from gaining rights under [Art 45 TFEU]. He was entitled to the same benefits as Dutch nationals.

9.3.6

Steymann v Staatssecretaris voor Justitie 196/87 [1988] ECR 6159

Key Facts

A member of a religious sect acted as a plumber for the group and received board and some 'pocket money' but no pay in return.

Key Law

The ECJ held that he could be classed as a worker as he was engaged in a genuine and effective activity which was an inherent commercial aspect of his membership of the group.

9.3.6

Hoekstra v Bestuur der Badrijfsvereniging voor Detailhandel en Ambachten 75/63 [1964] ECR 177

Key Facts

A Dutch national fell ill while visiting her parents in Germany and sought to claim back the cost of treatment when she returned to the Netherlands.

Key Law

The ECJ held that she should succeed. The Court identified that the term 'worker' should be broadly interpreted and this should include a person who has lost a job but is capable of getting another.

Key Comment

This and the cases above demonstrate how broadly the ECJ is prepared to define the term 'worker'.

9.3.6

R v Immigration Appeal Tribunal ex p Antonissen 292/89 [1991] ECR I-745

Key Facts

A Belgian national who had been resident in the UK and looking for work for two years challenged a deportation order following his conviction for possession of cocaine. Under UK law non-nationals could be deported after six months without work.

Key Law

The ECJ held that work-seekers were protected under [Art 45 TFEU] as much as those who had work. However, it also held that six months was an adequate time limit and would not be in breach of [Art 45 TFEU].

Key Link

Procureur du Roi v Royer 48/75 [1976] ECR 497 p 69.

9.3.6

Trojani v Le Centre Public d'Aide Sociale de Bruxelles C-456/02 [2004] All ER (EC) 1065

Key Facts

A French national moved to Belgium and lived in campsites and youth hostels. While resident in a Salvation Army hostel he received board and pocket money in return for completing various odd jobs as part of a personal socio-occupational reintegration programme.

Key Law

The ECJ held that this activity was capable of falling within the scope of [Art 45 TFEU] but was for the national court to determine.

Key Judgment

The Court said: 'The national court must ascertain whether the services actually performed are capable of being regarded as forming part of the normal labour market.' It distinguished Bettray *(see next case).*

9.3.7   *Bettray v Staatssecretaris van Justitie* 344/87 [1989] ECR 1621

Key Facts

A German national, living in the Netherlands, was on a state-sponsored drug rehabilitation scheme.

Key Law

The ECJ held that he was not a worker as there was no genuine economic activity involved.

9.4.2   *Netherlands State v Anne Florence Reed* 59/85 [1986] ECR 1283

Key Facts

Reed, a UK national, went to join her partner, another UK national, who lived in the Netherlands. When she applied for a residence permit this was refused because she had not yet found work.

Key Law

The ECJ held that, as a co-habitee, she could not come within the definition of worker's family in [Art 2(1) Directive 2004/38], which refers to 'spouse'. However, the court did recognise that it was possible for a worker to have a co-habitee living with him as a 'social advantage' under Art 7(2) of Regulation 1612/68, since the same social advantage could be enjoyed by workers of the host state, and to deny this right to the migrant worker would be discrimination.

Key Problem

The definition of family originally in Art 10 Regulation 1612/68 was clearly narrow and had the potential to discriminate against certain relationships. This has been overcome by Directive 2004/38, the Citizens' Free Movement Rights Directive, which repeals Art 10 of Regulation 1612/68. Art 2(2)(b) redefnes 'family member' as including a 'partner [under] a registered partnership', taking into account civil marriages. Art 3(2)(b) also allows entry and residence rights to a partner 'with whom the EU citizen has a durable relationship'.

9.4.3   *Diatta v Land Berlin* 267/83 [1985] ECR 567

Key Facts

A Senegalese woman and her French husband had settled in Germany and some time later separated. When she applied for renewal of her work permit she was refused on the ground that she was no longer a member of a worker's family.

Key Law

The ECJ held that her rights under Regulation 1612/68 would not end until the marriage was lawfully terminated.

Key Judgment

The ECJ recognised that 'if co-habitation of the spouses were a mandatory condition, the worker could at any time cause the expulsion of his spouse by depriving her of a roof'.

9.5.3   *Procureur du Roi v Royer* 48/75 [1976] ECR 497

Key Facts

A French national was charged with entering Belgium illegally without a residence permit. He was refused the right to apply for a residence permit and given a deportation order with immediate effect, and with no right to appeal.

Key Law

The ECJ held that the right of residence did not depend on the issue of a permit. Under the derogations in Art 45(3) and [Directive 2004/38], a migrant should have the same remedies as those for workers of the host state and it would be anomalous to make the procedural rights and safeguards conditional on the presence of a permit.

Key Link

R v Pieck 157/79 [1980] ECR 2171, where the ECJ held that, although Member States are entitled to penalise a migrant not complying with administrative formalities, this can never justify deportation. This is now incorporated in Art 9(3) of Directive 2004/38.

9.6.2   *Commission v France (Re French Merchant Seamen)* 167/73 [1974] ECR 359

Key Facts

French maritime law required that French merchant ships should hire crew members at a ratio of three French to one other nationality. The Commission challenged this law as in breach of [Art 45 TFEU].

Key Law

The ECJ held that, despite the French argument that the law was no longer applied, it still breached Art 4(1) of Regulation 1612/68, guaranteeing equality in eligibility for employment and it would create an unacceptable ambiguity in the law if it was not repealed.

9.6.2   *Groener v Minister for Education* 397/87 [1989] ECR 3967

Key Facts

A Dutch national applied for a teaching post in Ireland and was rejected because she did not have a Certificate of Proficiency in the Irish language as required for all Irish teachers. She challenged this as the teaching was to be in English.

Key Law

The ECJ held that the Irish law was justified under Art 3(1) of Regulation 1612/68 since language was an important part of the culture of any state and there was no discrimination as the same requirement was made of Irish nationals who may not have the required proficiency in the language either.

9.6.2

Wurttembergische Milchvertung-Sudmilch AG v Ugliola 15/69 [1969] ECR 363

Key Facts

A German employer, in determining the seniority of staff, took into account periods of national service in Germany. Ugliola completed national service in Italy, which was not taken into account.

Key Law

The ECJ held that this was a breach of Art 7(1) of the regulation; requiring that migrant workers must not be subject to differences in conditions, pay, dismissal, etc. from the workers of the host state.

9.6.2

Sotgiu v Deutsche Bundespost 152/73 [1974] ECR 153

Key Facts

The German post office paid a separation allowance for workers who were forced to live away from their families. This was 10 DM for those whose family home was in Germany but only 7.5 DM for those whose family home was elsewhere.

Key Law

The ECJ held that German nationals were much more likely to qualify for the higher allowance so the measure was discriminatory.

9.6.2

Fiorini v SNCF 32/75 [1975] ECR 1085

Key Facts

The widow of an Italian railway worker who had worked in France for SNCF was denied special fare reductions granted to large families. The French restricted rights to social advantages to those gaining them within employment and the widow had never worked.

Key Law

The ECJ held that Art 7(2) of Regulation 1612/68 covered all social and tax advantages, whether gained through employment or not. These rights continued after the worker's death and it would be discrimination on nationality to deny them to the widow.

Key Comment

The ECJ rightly recognised that Art 7 cannot be interpreted narrowly otherwise it would promote inequality.

9.6.2

Centre Public d'Aide Sociale Courcelles v Lebon 316/85 [1987] ECR 2811

Key Facts

Lebon was the child of French parents working in Belgium, was born in Belgium and had lived there for all but two years. On her return to Belgium, by which time her parents were retired, she was given income support but this was withdrawn on the basis that she was not seeking work. She was 24 at the time.

Key Law

The ECJ identified that, while children of a worker cease to be classed as family on reaching 21, they do not lose family status if still dependent. Dependency does not cease merely because the child makes a claim for benefit. Otherwise this would mean that no member of a worker's family, other than a spouse and a child under 21, could ever make such a claim and remain a family member.

Key Judgment

The Court stated: 'The status of dependent . . . is a factual situation . . . and there is no need to determine the reasons for recourse to the worker's support or to raise the question whether the person is able to support himself by taking up paid employment.'

9.6.2

Gul v Regierungspresident Düsseldorf 131/85 [1986] ECR 1573

Key Facts

A Cypriot national, with Turkish medical qualifications, married an English woman working in Germany. He had long-term temporary work as an anaesthetist, gained German qualifications and applied to practise medicine in Germany but was refused on his nationality.

Key Law

The ECJ held that Art 11 of Regulation 1612/68 gave family members the right to employment on the same basis as nationals and as such the only requirement was that he had the appropriate qualifications, which he did. The refusal was discrimination.

9.6.2

Michel S v Fonds national de reclassement des handicappes 76/72 [1973] ECR 457

Key Facts

The mentally handicapped son of an Italian national employed in Belgium before his death was denied a benefit for people whose job prospects were affected by disability.

Key Law

The ECJ held that Art 12 of the Regulation entitled non-nationals to the same educational benefits as nationals including rehabilitation benefits.

9.6.2

Casagrande v Landeshauptstadt Munchen 9/74 [1974] ECR 773

Key Facts

The son of a deceased Italian who had worked in Germany was refused an educational grant.

Key Law

The ECJ held that Art 12 of the Regulation entitles the children of migrant workers not only to the same access to education as nationals of the host state but also to measures that support education such as grants.

9.6.2

GBC Echtemach and Moritz v Netherlands Minister for Education 389/87 & 390/87 [1989] ECR 723

Key Facts

In joined references Moritz, a German national, went to live in the Netherlands with his father who worked there, rather than remain with his mother. They then returned to Germany but the son applied to complete his education in the Netherlands and was refused.

Key Law

The ECJ held that his access to education under Art 12 of the Regulation was not diminished by his father's return to Germany.

9.6.2

Forcheri v Belgian State 152/82 [1983] ECR 2323

Key Facts

The wife of an Italian EC (now EU) official in Belgium gained a place on a social work training course but was required to pay a 'minerval' (a supplementary fee that was imposed on foreign students but not Belgian students) as all non-nationals were.

Key Law

The ECJ held that, since she was legally resident in Belgium, the imposition was a breach of Art 12 of the regulation, discrimination on nationality.

Key Comment

The decision could also be seen as arising out of her status as the spouse of a worker under Regulation 1612/68.

9.6.2

Landesamt fur Ausbildungsforderung Nordrhein Westfalen v Gaal C-7/94 [1995] ECR I-1031

Key Facts

Gaal was born in Belgium but brought up in Germany, later studying at a German university. At age 22 he applied for funding to study at a British university. German authorities rejected his claim since his father had died and he was not financially dependent on his mother.

Key Law

The ECJ held that the definition of 'child' for the purposes of access to education under Art 12 of Regulation 1612/68 could not be subject to the same conditions of dependency as was the definition used to establish if the child was a family member of the worker, so Gaal could challenge the refusal.

Key Judgment

The Court said that 'to make the application of Art 12 subject to an age limit or to the status of dependent child would conflict not only with the letter of that provision, but also with its spirit'.

9.6.2

Lair v Universität Hannover 39/86 [1989] ECR 3161

Key Facts

A French national had worked intermittently in Germany with periods of voluntary unemployment. She gained a place to study languages and literature at Hanover University but her application for a maintenance grant was rejected because of a rule, only applied to non-nationals, that she had not worked for a complete five-year period prior to the application.

Key Law

The ECJ held that she was still a worker and under Art 7(1) of the Regulation was entitled to the same funding as nationals.

9.6.2

Givane v Secretary of State for the Home Department C-257/00 [2003] ECR I-345

Key Facts

A Portuguese national lived and worked in the UK for three years before leaving for India for ten months and returning to the UK with his Indian wife and three children. He died 21 months later. UK authorities refused the family the right to remain after his death because he had not resided continuously for at least two years.

Key Law

The ECJ held that the right under Regulation 1251/70 (now replaced by Directive 2004/38) must refer to the period immediately preceding the worker's death and could not be applied to the former period. This was because the rule was intended to establish a significant connection between the worker and his family and the state and to ensure a level of integration.

9.8.3

Bosman v Royal Belgian Football Association and UEFA C-415/93 [1995] ECR I-4921

Key Facts

Bosman, a professional footballer with Liège FC in Belgium, was prevented from joining a new football club in France after expiry of his contract because of UEFA rules, which meant that he could not transfer without Liège receiving a fee from the French club. Liège set this too high for the French club to agree to and in effect prevented Bosman from working.

Key Law

The ECJ held that the imposition of transfer fees for out-of-contract players was an unjustifiable restriction on their [Art 45 TFEU] rights.

Key Comment

The ruling has had a major impact on the football transfer system and also on the numbers of non-nationals playing in national leagues.

9.10.4   *Van Duyn v The Home Office* 41/74 [1974] ECR 1337

Key Facts

A Dutch national and member of the Church of Scientology was offered a position in the Church in the UK but was refused entry by immigration officials on the grounds that the government had declared members of the church as undesirables, although the Church was not banned in the UK. They argued that her rights were exempted under the derogation in [Art 45(3) TFEU] and Directive [2004/38].

Key Law

The ECJ recognised that the derogations of public policy and public security must, according to Art 3(1) of the directive, be based exclusively on the personal conduct of the individual concerned, but that membership of an organisation may constitute personal conduct. However, the Court did distinguish between past and present membership. It added that personal conduct can be sufficient to justify either deportation or refusal of entry.

Key Comment

The decision is significant in that it gives Member States the means to legally expel people who are members of terrorist groups.

9.10.4   *Rutili v Ministere de l'Intérieur* 36/75 [1975] ECR 1219

Key Facts

An Italian political activist was restricted in his movement by an order of the French Minister and challenged this order.

Key Law

The ECJ held that, in order for the derogation of public policy to apply, the individual must constitute a genuine and serious threat. Also the grounds for the restriction on movement must be indicated in a clear and comprehensive statement so that the person can prepare an adequate defence to the decision.

9.10.5

R v Bouchereau 30/77 [1978] ECR 1999

Key Facts

A French national working in the UK was convicted of possession of drugs and given a suspended sentence. He was later charged again for possession and the magistrate contemplated a recommendation for an immediate deportation order.

Key Law

The ECJ held that deportation, using the public policy or public security derogations, was permissible only if the person posed a genuine and serious threat to society.

Key Judgment

The Court held that 'The existence of a previous criminal conviction can . . . only be taken into account in so far as the circumstances which gave rise to that conviction are evidence of personal conduct constituting a present threat to the requirements of public policy'.

9.10.5

Bonsignore v Oberstadtdirecktor of the City of Cologne 67/74 [1975] ECR 297

Key Facts

An Italian national working in Germany accidentally shot his brother. He was convicted of illegal possession of a firearm and was ordered to be deported.

Key Law

The ECJ held that deportation could not occur using the derogation as justification merely in order to act as a deterrent.

9.10.5   *Adoui and Cornaille v Belgian State* 115/81 & 116/81 [1982] ECR 1665

Key Facts

Two French women were employed as waitresses in a bar in Belgium and were also prostitutes. They were refused residence permits because it was shown that they sat in windows semi-naked.

Key Law

The ECJ held that public policy only applies if Member States take similar repressive measures against their own nationals for similar behaviour. Since similar behaviour was subject only to small fines for nationals the derogation was being applied disproportionately.

9.11.2   *Commission v Belgium (Re Public Employees)* 149/79 [1980] ECR 3881

Key Facts

A Belgian law reserved posts in the public service for Belgian nationals. The law included posts as diverse as nurses and plumbers employed by local authorities.

Key Law

The ECJ held that the public service in [Art 45(4) TFEU] could not apply. This was reserved for posts involving the exercise of public authority in order to safeguard the general interests of the state.

Key Link

Commission v France (Re French Nurses) 307/84 [1985] ECR 1725.

10 Art 49 and freedom of establishment; Art 56 and the right to provide services

Art 49 and freedom of establishment

- Grants individuals the right to establish a profession or business in another Member State, or to set up an agency, branch or subsidiary.
- Art 49 is directly applicable, so no need to introduce directives (*Reyners v The Belgian State*).
- It is also directly effective and has been applied, e.g. to lawyers (*Thieffrey v Conseil a l'Ordre des Avocates a la court de Paris*).
- The main obstacle is national qualifications.
- Three methods are used to resolve this problem:
  - i) harmonisation through individual directives;
  - ii) ECJ developed principle of equivalence of qualifications;
  - iii) mutual recognition originally under Directive 89/48. Now these are incorporated in Directive 2005/36, the Recognition of Professional Qualifications Directive.

RIGHTS OF ESTABLISHMENT AND PROVISION OF SERVICES

Freedom to provide services:

- Art 56 appropriate for those wishing to provide services without settling in the host nation.
- By Art 57 these are services of an industrial and commercial character, craftsmanship and the exercise of a profession.
- Right is directly effective, so claimants subject to same rules as national (*Van Binsbergen v Bestuur van de Bedrijfsvereniging voor de Metaalnijverheid*).
- Right is also to receive as well as to provide services (*Luisi and Carbone v Ministero del Tesoro*).
- But right requires an economic element (*SPUC v Grogan*).

❿ 10.1 Introduction

1   Both rights were essential to the creation of a single market.

2   The right to establish is contained in Arts 49–54:

- It refers to the right of free movement of both the self-employed and professionals.

- It can include 'legal' as well as natural persons.

- It is the right to set up and carry out a business, trade or profession in another Member State.

3   The freedom to provide services is in Arts 56–62. It complements the right of establishment by allowing a person established in one state to exercise a business or profession in another state, not linked to residence.

4   The difference between establishment and providing services was identified in *Gebhard* C-55/94 – establishment is where the person participates 'on a stable and continuous basis' whereas providing a service is pursuing an activity 'on a temporary basis'.

5   There is an obvious overlap between the two principles, and some similarity with Art 45 – and both are subject to the same derogations in Directive 2004/38, which also provides rights of entry and residence.

6   In either case the requirement is that the person should be subject to the same condition as nationals.

7   The major barrier to the freedoms is national qualifications or requirements.

❿ 10.2 Freedom of establishment

1   Art 49 provides that 'restrictions on the freedom of establishment of nationals of one member state in the territory of another shall be prohibited . . . such prohibition shall also apply to restrictions on the setting up of agencies, branches or subsidiaries . . .'.

2   Art 49 is directly applicable, so introducing Directives is not vital (*Reyners v The Belgian State* 2/74); although harmonising directives was the means anticipated for dealing with the problem of different qualifications in different Member States.

3   It is also directly effective, so can be applied in a variety of circumstances:

- *Thieffrey v Conseil a l'Ordre des Avocates a la cour de Paris* 71/76 and lawyers;

- *Patrick v Ministre des Affaires Culturelles* 11/77 and architects;

- *Van Ameyde v Ufficio Centrale Italiano di Assistenza Assiscurativa Automobilisti in Circolazione Internazionale* 90/76 and a motor insurance claims investigator.

4   The main barrier to the freedoms is national regulation of trades and professions based on national qualifications.

5   Three methods were devised to resolve this problem:

- harmonisation of professional qualifications through 'sectoral' Directives;

- 'mutual recognition' of qualifications by Directive 89/48, Directive 92/51 and the 'Slim' Directive 2001/19;

- 'equivalence' of qualifications using the principle of non-discrimination; now these have been incorporated in Directive 2005/36, the Recognition of Professional Qualifications Directive.

6   Harmonisation was achieved only by a complex, time-consuming process of introducing individual directives for individual trades, e.g.:

- retail trade and Directive 68/363;

- doctors and Directive 93/16;

- architects and Directive 85/384;

- lawyers and Directive 77/249 (but only limited rights to practice).

The effect was that a person qualified in one state could then automatically practise in another.

7   Mutual recognition was developed because harmonisation was too time consuming and impossible in certain areas. Directive 89/48 introduced a general system for mutual recognition of 'higher education diplomas':

- These are qualifications taking three years or more.

- The directive applies if no harmonising directive exists.

- This means that Member States must assess the equivalence of qualifications of other states so that a person can establish without needing to re-qualify.

- However, a substantial difference can lead to requirement of an aptitude test or an adaptation period.

- This was supplemented by Directive 92/51 in respect of one-year year vocational qualifications.

- And since then by the Slim Directive 2001/19 requiring Member States to take into account work experience and qualifications gained in third countries.

8   Where there is no harmonising directive and mutual recognition cannot apply the principle of non-discrimination can be used: *Steinhauser v City of Biarritz* 197/84, *Klopp* 107/83, *Gebhard* C-55/94 and the established principles in, e.g., *Reyners, Thieffrey, Patrick:*

●   the Member State must assess the equivalency of the person's qualifications (*UNECTEF v Heylens* 222/86);

●   and must give reasons why not and allow appeal (*Vlassopoulou* C-340/89).

9   Directive 2005/36 has incorporated the sectoral directives and introduced a new simpler and fairer process of mutual recognition of qualifications. In respect of the principle of non-discrimination formerly developed in the case law, where either sectoral directives or mutual recognition do not apply, there is a requirement of non-discrimination and proportionality.

●   Arts 10–15 provide for a general system of recognition of professional qualifications – so acts as a fall-back for qualifications falling outside of the previous processes – obviously adaptation tests/periods still apply;

●   Arts 16–20 provide an automatic system of recognition based on prior professional experience in certain defined areas;

●   Arts 21–49 provide a system of automatic recognition of qualification in specific professions, e.g. doctors, nurses, dentists, vets, midwives, pharmacists and architects.

▌ 10.3 The freedom to provide and receive services

1   Art 56 provides for the abolition of restrictions on the freedom to provide services by non-nationals who are not established in the state of the recipient. So it is designed for those wishing to provide services without settling in the host nation.

2   Services are identified in Art 57 as those normally provided for remuneration, not related to free movement of capital, goods or workers, 'of an industrial and commercial character, craftsmanship and the exercise of a profession . . .'.

3   The right is directly effective:

●   so claimants are subject to the same rules of professional conduct as nationals (*Van Binsbergen v Bestuur van de Bedrijfsvereniging voor de Metaalnijverheid* 33/74);

- but the right can be denied only where there is an imperative reason of public interest (*Omega* C-36/02).

4   The important corollary of the rule is the enforceable freedom to receive services (*Luisi and Carbone v Ministero del Tesoro* 286/82):

- this principle has been extended to cover access to education and vocational training (*Gravier v City of Liege* 293/83);

- so vocational courses must be offered on equal terms to all EU citizens (*Blaizot v University of Liege* 24/86);

- but state, secondary education is not a service (*Belgium v Humbel* 263/86);

- and maintenance grants are outside of the scope of the article (*Brown v Secretary of State for Scotland* 197/86).

5   The principle of non-discrimination has been extended further to include receipt of state compensation (*Cowan v French Treasury* 186/87).

6   However, this is unavailable without an economic element (*SPUC v Grogan* C-159/80).

Key Cases Checklist

Reyners v The Belgian State (1974)
Art 49 is directly applicable, so no need to introduce Directives and can be directly effective – and the case succeeded because of Art 18: no discrimination based on nationality
Gebhard v Milan Bar Council (1995)
National measures must be proportionate to the object to be achieved

---

**Rights of Establishment
Provision of Services,
Receiving Services**

Freedom to provide services

Van Binsbergen v Bestuur van de Bedrijfsvereniging voor de Metaalnijverheid (1974)
Art 56 is directly effective so migrants are subject to the same rule as nationals
Luisi and Carbone v Ministero del Tesoro (1984)
The right is to receive as well as to provide services
SPUC v Grogan (1991)
But the right requires an economic element

10.2.2

Reyners v The Belgian State 2/74 [1974] ECR 631

Key Facts

Reyners was a Dutch national, resident in Belgium and qualified to practise Belgian law. He was being prevented from joining the Belgian bar because of a law requiring practising lawyers to be Belgian nationals. Belgium was arguing that, since [Art 49 TFEU] was to be implemented by the introduction of 'sectoral' Directives, it failed the third test from *Van Gend en Loos*; it was conditional, and therefore not directly effective and could not be relied upon or enforced.

Key Law

The ECJ held that, since Member States were to eliminate barriers to rights of establishment by the end of the transitional period, which had passed, and since [Art 49 TFEU] was sufficiently clear and precise, it was directly effective. Besides this, the measure was a straightforward breach of the requirement in [Art 18 TFEU] for there to be no discrimination based on nationality.

10.2.3

Thieffrey v Conseil a l'Ordre des Avocates a la cour de Paris 71/76 [1977] ECR 765

Key Facts

A Belgian national with a doctorate in law who had also practised in Belgium had his qualifications accepted by a French university which awarded him the necessary Certificate of Aptitude for practice as a lawyer in France. However, the Paris Bar rejected his application on the basis that he did not have a French law degree.

Key Law

The ECJ held that, following *Reyners*, this was a breach of [Art 49 TFEU], despite the fact that there was no harmonising Directive on professional legal qualifications at that time.

10.2.3

Patrick v Ministre des Affaires Culturelles 11/77 [1977] ECR 1199

Key Facts

An English architect wished to establish in France but was prevented from doing so. Again there was no harmonising Directive for the profession. However, a French Ministerial Decree of 1964 had recognised the English qualifications as corresponding to the French ones.

Key Law

The ECJ held that the refusal to deny Patrick a right to establish was purely discrimination based on nationality and breached [Art 49 TFEU].

10.2.8

Steinhauser v City of Biarritz 197/84 [1985] ECR 1819

Key Facts

A German artist who was resident in France was prevented from exhibiting paintings in a crampotte (a fisherman's hut). A local law stated that the huts could only be rented by French nationals.

Key Law

The ECJ held that, even though the law in effect gave advantages to French nationals rather than being an outright bar to establishment, it was still direct discrimination and breached [Art 49 TFEU].

10.2.8

Paris Bar Council v Klopp 107/83 [1984] ECR 2971

Key Facts

A German national, and member of the Dusseldorf Bar, applied for membership of the Paris Bar, wishing to set up chambers there as well as in Germany. He was rejected because of Paris Bar Council rules requiring avocats to establish chambers in only one place, the justification being that the rule was necessary to ensure adequate contact between lawyer and client.

Key Law

The ECJ concluded that the measure was not proportionate since both transport and communication links were efficient and effective and a less restrictive measure could have been employed instead.

Key Judgment

The ECJ stated: 'Such a restrictive interpretation would mean that a lawyer once established in a particular Member State would be able to enjoy the freedom . . . to establish in another Member State only at the price of abandoning the establishment he already had.'

10.2.8 ***Vlassopoulou v Ministerio fur Justiz***
C-340/89 [1991] ECR I-2357

Key Facts

A Greek national, qualified to practise in Greece, gained work in a German law firm with authorisation to advise on Greek and [EU] law. When she applied to join the German Bar she was refused on the grounds of lack of appropriate qualifications.

Key Law

The ECJ held that the German authorities were obliged to assess the equivalence of her Greek qualifications and to be given a reasoned decision for the refusal as well as the right to appeal.

Key Link

Directive 89/48, which provides for 'mutual recognition' of qualifications of three years at HE level, while allowing adaptation tests or periods. Directive 2001/19, which requires an appeals process and recognition of qualifications gained in third states (both Directives are now subsumed in Directive 2005/36, The Recognition of Professional Qualifications Directive).

10.2.8

Gebhard v Milan Bar Council C-55/94 [1995] ECR I-4165

Key Facts

The Milan Bar brought disciplinary proceedings against Gebhard, a German lawyer, for using the term *'avvocato'*, a title reserved for those possessing Italian legal professional qualifications.

Key Law

The ECJ held that, because of the amount of time he had spent in Milan, he had established himself there and was entitled to rely on [Art 49 TFEU]. The national measures should be applied in a non-discriminatory manner, be justified by imperative requirements in the general interest, be suitable and proportionate to attain the objective. Since the measure was to protect clients from unscrupulous people who passed themselves off as qualified lawyers it was justifiable in the circumstances.

10.3.3

Van Binsbergen v Bestuur van de Bedrijfsvereniging voor de Metaalnijverheid 33/74 [1974] ECR 1299

Key Facts

Dutch rules required lawyers to be habitually resident before they could practise. This prevented a legal adviser from representing his client when the client moved to Belgium.

Key Law

The ECJ held that this infringed [Art 56 TFEU] rights of freedom to provide services in another Member State by depriving them of all useful effect. It would discriminate against foreign nationals who would be less likely to be permanently resident.

Key Comment

Art 56 means that a person wishing to offer professional services in another state, while not establishing, is subject to the same rules of professional conduct as professionals in the host state. The right to offer services can only be denied where there is an imperative reason of public interest. The case also identifies that Art 56 is directly effective in the same way as Art 49.

10.3.3   *Omega* C-36/02 [2005] 1 CMLR 5

Key Facts

A German company operated a 'laserdome' (where customers shot at each other with laser-guided guns aimed at 'laser tags' that they wore). It used equipment bought from a British company. Local police successfully applied for an order to ban the activity as it was contrary to a German constitutional law prohibiting 'acts of simulated homicide and the trivialisation of violence' in order to preserve respect for human dignity.

Key Law

The ECJ held that the German law infringed the British company's [Art 56 TFEU] rights to provide services, but the law was justified under the Art 46 derogation of public policy, public security or public health.

10.3.4   *Luisi and Carbone v Ministero del Tesoro* 286/82 and 26/83 [1984] ECR 377

Key Facts

Two Italian nationals were prosecuted under an Italian law making it illegal to take more than a set amount of money out of the country. Both had taken large sums elsewhere for purposes of tourism and one had also done so for medical treatment. They were fined the differences between the amounts they were allowed to take out of the country and the legal amount under Italian law. They challenged the law as being in breach of [Art 56 TFEU].

Key Law

The ECJ held that an important corollary of the right to provide services was the right also to receive services, without which [Art 56 TFEU] would be ineffective. There was a breach of [Art 56 TFEU].

Key Judgment

The Court stated that 'The freedom to provide services includes the freedom, for the recipient of services, to go to another Member State in order to receive a service there, without being obstructed ... and ... tourists, persons receiving medical treatment and persons travelling for the purpose of education or business are to be regarded as recipients of services'.

10.3.4

Gravier v City of Liège 293/83 [1985] ECR 593

Key Facts

A French art student was accepted for a four-year course at the academy in Liege in Belgium and refused to pay the 'minerval' (a supplementary fee that was imposed on foreign students but not Belgian students) and claimed that the fee breached [Art 18 TFEU].

Key Law

The ECJ accepted that the course could be classed as vocational training, bringing it within the scope of [Art 18 TFEU] and meaning that the foreign students were indeed being discriminated against.

Key Link

Blaizot v University of Liège 24/86 [1988] ECR 379, in which the ECJ made basically the same point in respect of university courses which the state had challenged as being academic not vocational.
Belgium v Humbel 263/86 [1988] ECR 5365, where the ECJ made it clear that while privately funded education is covered by [Art 56 TFEU], state-funded education cannot be classed as vocational and is not.
Brown v Secretary of State for Scotland 197/86 [1988] ECR 3205, which held that maintenance grants fell outside the scope of [Art 56 TFEU].

10.3.5

Cowan v French Treasury 186/87 [1989] ECR 195

Key Facts

Cowan, an English tourist, was assaulted and robbed on the Metro in Paris. He applied for compensation from the French equivalent of the Criminal Injuries Compensation Board but was denied because French law reserved this for only French nationals.

Key Law

The ECJ held that, in effect, this law obstructed his right to move freely to France and receive services (tourism) so was a breach of his rights under [Art 56 TFEU].

10.3.6

Society for the Protection of Unborn Children (SPUC) v Grogan C-159/90 [1991] ECR I-4685

Key Facts

The Irish Constitution recognised the right to life of foetuses and other law made abortion illegal, meaning that women wishing to have abortions were forced to travel elsewhere. Grogan, a student, published information on where female students could obtain abortions in London and when the SPUC gained an injunction from the Irish High Court to prevent publication, he challenged the Irish law as being in breach of his [Art 56 TFEU] rights to provide services.

Key Law

The ECJ avoided declaring on the issue of the compatibility of the Irish Constitution and [Art 56 TFEU] by stating that the link between the abortions and the information Grogan had given was too tenuous for his activity to be called a service. Besides this there was no economic activity involved so there was no breach of [Art 56 TFEU].

11 EU competition law

▶ 11.1 The purpose and character of competition law

11.1.1 The purpose of competition law

1 Art 4 TEU [originally Art 2 EC Treaty] sees the task of EU law as 'the promotion of harmonious development of economic activities by the creation of a common market and the progressive approximation of the economic policies of the Member States . . .'.

2 The EU is also bound to ensure that 'competition in the internal market is not distorted . . .'.

3 So, the framers of the original Treaty:

- recognised that unfettered market forces can lead directly to anti-competitive practices;

- inserted rules to deal with this based on the Sherman Act model.

4 These rules had three principal objectives:

- to avoid restrictive practices and agreements (Art 101);

- to prevent large businesses from abusing their market dominance (Art 102);

- to apply similar rules to the public sector (Art 106).

5 EU competition law is criticised because:

- all practices are treated alike, even if they would benefit the consumer;

- policy has been said to sacrifice equity and efficiency to political goals;

- Ian Ward says its existence is 'a perversity' and 'the loud admission of defeat' and 'an admission that the market alone cannot effect competition';

- there is always the danger of Member States clinging to national interests.

6   But the EU has succeeded in framing cohesive and consistent objectives, identified in the Commission's Ninth Report on Competition Policy:

- creation of an open and unified market not partitioned by restrictive and anti-competitive agreements;

- realisation of effective competition avoiding over-concentration or abuses by dominant companies;

- achieving fairness in the market place, giving support to small and medium-sized firms, protecting the consumer, and penalising unlawful state subsidies;

- maintaining the competitive position of the EU against rivals in the global economy.

11.1.2 The character of competition law

1   It covers everything – goods, services and intellectual property rights.

2   Provisions are framed in broad terms, so are subject to ECJ interpretation.

3   It can be used against firms regardless of existence of registered office in the EU.

4   Rules are pragmatic, so are subject to exceptions to preserve market efficiency.

5   Penalties apply where trade in the EU is affected, so can apply to small firms and inter-state disputes.

6   So it is possible for EU law and national law to co-exist (*Wilhelm v Bundeskartellamt* 14/68).

7   Art 101 and Art 102 are complementary, pursuing the same objectives by focusing on different types of activity.

The basic Art 101 prohibition:

- Rule prohibits 'agreements between undertakings, decisions of associations of undertakings and concerted practices which may affect trade between Member States having as object prevention, restriction or distortion of competition within internal market'.
- Undertakings defined by ECJ as 'single organisation of personal, tangible and intangible elements, attached to an autonomous legal entity and pursuing a long-term economic aim' (*Mannesmann v High Authority*), e.g. a trade association (*FRUBO v Commission*).
- Commission can grant exemption.

ART 101 AND RESTRICTIVE PRACTICES

Activities beyond scope of Art 101:

Commission Notice on agreement of minor importance:
- if less than 10% market share for horizontal agreements; 15% for vertical agreements;
- commercial agents and subsidiaries.

Exemptions if:
- contributes to improving production or distribution of goods or promoting technical or economic progress (*Transocean Marine Paint Association*);
- consumer gets fair share of benefit (*ACEC v Berliet*);
- no unnecessary restrictions (*Consten and Grundig v Commission*);
- no risk of eliminating competition (*Re Fine Papers*);
- can be individual or block.

Elements proving breach of Art 101:

Agreements between undertakings, decisions by associations of undertakings, concerted practices:
- must involve collusive behaviour (*AEG Telefunken v Commission*);
- decisions by associations of undertakings are usually by trade associations on, e.g. fixing discounts, collective boycotts, restrictive contract clauses;
- concerted practices are a form of co-ordination between enterprises that has not yet reached the point where it is a contract (*ICI Ltd v Commission (The Dyestuffs Case)*);
- Art 101 identifies some prohibited arrangements, e.g.:
  - i) price fixing (*VBVB and VVVB v Commission*);
  - ii) limiting production (*The Quinine Cartel case*);
  - iii) sharing markets or suppliers (*Siemens/Fanuc*);
  - iv) applying dissimilar conditions to equivalent transactions (*IAZ International Belgium*).

Affecting trade between Member States:
- ascertained by reference to free movement and attainment of single market;
- must be capable of constituting a threat, direct or indirect, actual or potential, on the pattern of trade (*Belasco v Commission*);
- no need to prove harm, just that agreement may prevent, restrict or distort competition sufficiently (*Vereeniging van Cementhandelaren v Commission*).

Object or effect of preventing, restricting or distorting competition:
- as much to do with practical outcomes as intentions;
- key issue is whether or not competition is affected (*Consten and Grundig v Commission*);
- ECJ try to apply the rules so as not to stifle enterprise and initiative (*Société Technique Minière v Maschinenbau Ulm*).

▶ 11.2 Art 101 and restrictive practices

11.2.1 The basic prohibition in Art 101

1   By Art 101, 'All agreements between undertakings, decisions of associations of undertakings and concerted practices which may affect trade between Member States and which have as their object or effect the prevention, restriction or distortion of competition within the internal market' are prohibited.

2   Art 101 also gives particular examples of anti-competitive acts – those which:

● directly or indirectly fix purchase or selling prices or any other trading conditions;

● limit or control production, markets, technical development or investment;

● share markets or sources of supply;

● apply dissimilar conditions to equivalent transactions with other trading parties, thereby placing them at a competitive disadvantage;

● make the conclusion of contracts subject to acceptance by the other parties of supplementary obligations which, by their nature, have no connection with the subject of such contracts.

3   Art 101(2) makes all such agreements void. The Commission formerly granted exemptions and negative clearance; now the process of applying exemptions is internally dealt with within the Member State.

4   Both Art 101 and Art 102 concern conduct of 'undertakings'.

● The term is not defined in the Treaty, but is given a broad definition by the ECJ: 'a single organisation of personal, tangible and intangible elements, attached to an autonomous legal entity and pursuing a long term economic aim . . .' (*Mannesmann v High Authority* (1962)).

● It can therefore cover everything from an individual to a multi-national corporation.

● It has included, for example:

i)   an opera singer (*Re Unitel* 78/516);

ii)   a sports federation (*Re World Cup 1990 Package Tours Decision* 92/521);

iii) a state-owned corporation (*Italian State v Sacchi* 155/73);

iv)   a public agency (*Hofner v Macroton* C-41/90);

v)   a trade association (*FRUBO v Commission* 71/74);

- but must involve some form of economic activity (*FENIN v Commission* T-319/99) but the Court of Justice has taken a different view in relation to the International Olympic Committee (*Meca-Medina and Macjen v Commission* C-519/04P).

11.2.2 The elements of proof for an action under Art 101

Agreements between undertakings, decisions by associations of undertakings, concerted practices

1 Agreements: always involve some sort of collusive behaviour as distinct from unilateral acts (*AEG Telefunken v Commission* 107/82):

- can include informal, oral agreements (*Tepea* 28/77);

- and the so-called 'gentlemen's agreements' (*ACF Chemiefarma v Commission* 41, 44, 45/69 (*The Quinine Cartel Case*));

- but must involve autonomous behaviour – so not an agreement imposed by national law (*Commission and France v Ladbroke Racing Ltd* C359 and 379/95P).

2 Decisions by associations:

- usually involve rules of trade associations;

- and prohibited decisions would include: recommending prices, fixing discounts, collective boycotts, restrictive contract clauses;

- and even non-binding recommendations (*Vereeniging van Cementhandelaren v Commission* 8/72).

3 Concerted practices have been defined by the ECJ as: 'a form of co-ordination between enterprises that has not yet reached the point where it is a contract in the true sense of the word, but which, in practice, consciously substitutes co-operation for the risks of competition . . .' (*ICI Ltd v Commission* 48/69 (*The Dyestuffs Case*)).

- The Court of Justice has held that even a single meeting by undertakings can amount to a concerted practice (*T-Mobile Netherlands BV and Others v Raad van bestuur van der Nederlandse Mededingingsautoriteit* C-47/09).

4 The test is where parallel behaviour is co-operative, so lacks independence (*Co-operatieve Vereeniging 'Suiker Unie' v Commission* 40–48, 50, 54–56, 111, 113, 114/73 (*The Sugar Cartel Case*)).

5   Agreements may be:

- horizontal, i.e. between competitors, and may, for example, divide up markets (*The Dyestuffs Case*); or

- vertical, i.e. between undertakings at different levels in the process, and may be, for example, exclusive distribution arrangements, or licensing agreements.

6   The article identifies specific prohibited arrangements:

- Price fixing, which may be agreements on, for example, discounts, credit, etc., and have included:

  i) agreements between zinc producers (*Re Zinc Producers Group*);

  ii) agreements between Italian glass manufacturers (*Re Italian Flat Glass Cartel*);

  iii) a retail price maintenance agreement between Belgian and Dutch booksellers (*VBVB and VVVB v Commission* 43 and 63/82).

- Limiting production, where undertakings restrict their own growth to artificially raise prices and prevent outsiders entering the agreement (*The Quinine Cartel case*).

- Sharing markets or sources of supply:

  i) can involve carving up markets (either geographically or by product);

  ii) and is common in oligopolies where competitors give each other exclusive dealerships (*Siemens/Fanuc* 1985).

- Applying dissimilar conditions to equivalent transactions:

  i) to place another party at a disadvantage;

  ii) so might involve giving advantageous conditions to another party (*IAZ International Belgium* 96–102, 104, 105, 108, 110/82).

- Imposing supplementary obligations: those with no relationship with actual subject of contract.

Affecting trade between Member States

1   In order to breach Art 101 the agreement must affect trade between Member States.

2   This is ascertained by reference to the free movement of goods and attainment of a single market.

3   So it must be capable of constituting a threat 'direct or indirect, actual or potential, on the pattern of trade . . .' (*Belasco v Commission* 246/86).

4   So there is no need to prove actual harm as long as the agreement is likely to prevent, restrict or distort competition to a sufficient degree (*Vereeniging van Cementhandelaren v Commission* 8/72).

The object or effect of preventing, restricting or distorting competition

1   'Object' and 'effect' are clearly meant to be alternatives, so the test is as much to do with practical outcomes as intentions.

2   So the key issue is whether competition has been affected, not whether trade has gone up or down (*Consten and Grundig v Commission* 56 and 58/64).

3   The ECJ tries to apply the rules so as not to stifle enterprise and initiative (*Société Technique Miniere v Maschinenbau Ulm* 56/65).

4   It will also apply the *de minimis* rule (*Frans Volk v Etablissments Vervaecke Sprl* 5/69).

11.2.3 Activities falling outside of the scope of Art 101

1   Undertakings used to be able to obtain negative clearance or comfort letters from the Commission but now competition law is administered by national authorities.

2   Commission Notice on Minor Agreements 2001 – agreements not caught by Art 101 if less than a 10% market share for the goods or services in the area of the common market covered by the agreement if horizontal, or 15% if vertical – though a blacklist exists of agreements not tolerated whatever the level of effect.

3   Commercial relations to which the rules do not apply:

   ● commercial agents, where they are simply concerned with negotiating transactions for the principal, and assume no financial risk;

   ● subsidiaries and parent companies, as the subsidiary has no autonomous decision-making capacity (but may breach Art 102).

4   Exemptions:

- Art 101(3) creates criteria for exempting agreements.
- There are four conditions (two positive, two negative) to be met before exemption is granted:

    i) the agreement, decision or practice must contribute to improving production or distribution of goods or promoting technical or economic progress (*Transocean Marine Paint Association* (D1967) and *Re Vacuum Interrupters (No 1)* (D1977));

    ii) a fair share of the resulting benefit must accrue to the consumer, which is not merely the end consumer (*ACEC v Berliet* (D1968));

    iii) no unnecessary restrictions should be imposed, e.g. absolute territorial protections (*Consten and Grundig v Commission*);

    iv) there must be no possibility of the restrictions eliminating competition in respect of a substantial part of the product in question (*Re Fine Papers* (Decision 1972)).

- Individual exemptions used to be granted under Regulation 17/62 by notice to the Commission. Now under Regulation 1/2003 process is operated by Member States.
- Block exemptions:

    i) introduced to reduce the bureaucratic burden of applications for individual exemptions;

    ii) granted in Regulations covering specific types of agreements;

    iii) Examples include:

    - exclusive distribution: 1983/83;
    - exclusive purchasing: 1984/83;
    - patent licensing: 2349/84;
    - motor vehicle distribution: 123/85;
    - know-how licensing: 556/89;
    - Regulation 2790/99 exempts all vertical agreements except certain serious restraints;
    - research and development agreements: 2658/2000.

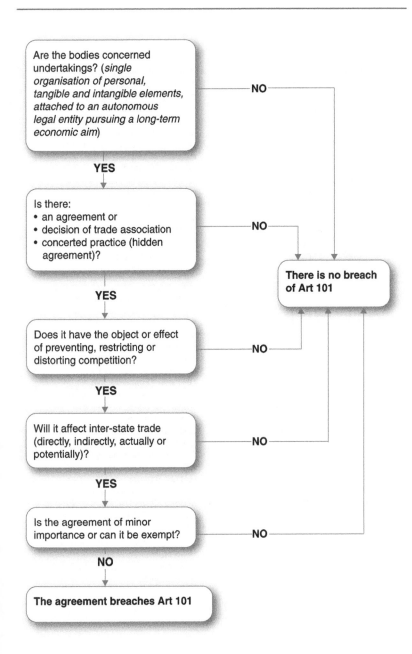

How a breach of Art 101 is established

The basic prohibition:

- Art 102 involves the concentration of economic power in an undertaking.
- Any abuse of commercial dominance is prohibited if it would affect trade between Member States.
- Art 102 can also apply to oligopolies (*The Flat Glass case*).
- Exemptions are not available (except for mergers).
- Three requirements:
    i) dominant position in market;
    ii) abuse of dominant position;
    iii) affects trade between Member States.

AN ART 102 ABUSE OF A DOMINANT POSITION

The abuse:

- Defined in case law as behaviour which influences structure of market so that competition is weakened, and maintenance or growth of competition is hindered.
- So could include, e.g.
- differential pricing for different Member States (*United Brands*);
- 'tying arrangements' (*Tetra Pak II*);
- dissimilar conditions;
- limiting markets, technical development, production (*Magill TV Guide & ITP v Commission*).

Affecting inter-state trade:

- must result from the abuse.

Existence of dominance:

- Dominance defined in ECSC Treaty – undertaking holds position shielding it against effective competition.
- The ECJ has also defined dominance and 'the power to control production or distribution for a significant part of the products in question' (*Continental Can Co. v Commission*) and 'a position of economic strength … which enables it to prevent competition being maintained' (*United Brands*).
- Need to consider:
    i) relevant market;
    ii) market share.

- Relevant product market decided on whether there is sufficient interchangeability between all the products forming part of the same market (*Hoffmann-la-Roche v Commission*).
- So could be, e.g. separate cartons for pasteurised and UHT milk (*Tetra Pak (No 1)*).
- Geographical market should be whole EU, but can take into account other factors, e.g. costs and feasibility of transport (*Hilti v Commission*).
- Temporal market may involve, e.g. seasonal factors (*United Brands*).
- No particular market share needed for dominance, e.g. 40% share in United Brands insufficient.
- Should consider, e.g.:
    i) market share *Hoffmann-la-Roche*);
    ii) competitor's share (*United Brands*).

▶ 11.3 Art 102 and abuse of a dominant position

11.3.1 Introduction

1   Art 101 concerns collusion between undertakings, but Art 102 usually concerns actions of a single undertaking.

2   So the threat to competition is the concentration of economic power.

3   By Art 102, 'Any abuse by one or more undertakings of a dominant position within the internal market or in a substantial part of it shall be prohibited as incompatible with the internal market insofar as it may affect trade between Member States':

- specific examples of abuses are identified;

- Art 101 and Art 102 are not mutually exclusive, so there is discretion which to claim under;

- Art 102 can apply also to oligopolies (*The Flat Glass Case* (D1989)).

4   Art 102 also deals with mergers and concentrations.

5   There are overlaps with Art 101 – exemptions are not available (though they are for mergers).

6   Art 102 does not prohibit dominant positions, only abuses, so is not meant to punish efficient economic behaviour.

7   There are three requirements that must be shown:

- that the undertaking has a dominant position in the market;

- that the practice in question abuses that dominant position;

- that trade between Member States is affected as a result.

11.3.2 The existence of a dominant position

1   Dominance is not defined in the Treaty, but it was in the ECSC Treaty where undertakings hold a position 'shielding them against effective competition in a substantial part of the [EU] . . .'

2   So it is left to the ECJ, as usual, to define in the cases:

- 'power to behave independently without taking into account their competitors, purchasers or suppliers because of their share of the market or . . . availability of technical knowledge, raw materials or capital, they have power to control production or distribution for significant part of products' (*Continental Can Co. v Commission* 6/72);

- 'a position of economic strength ... which enables it to prevent competition being maintained on the relevant market by giving it the power to behave to an appreciable effect independently of its competitors, and ultimately its consumers' (*United Brands v Commission 27/76*);

- 'such a position does not preclude some competition but enables (it) ... if not to determine, at least to have an appreciable effect on the conditions in which that competition will develop, and in any case to act largely in disregard of it' (*Hoffmann-la-Roche v Commission 85/76*).

3 So there are two key concepts in determining dominance:

- relevant product market and geographical market;

- calculation of market share.

The relevant product market

1 Dominant undertakings will want the product market defined broadly; those affected will want it to be defined narrowly.

2 So product market includes the product plus all products which may be perfectly substituted for it.

- It is measured on whether there is 'sufficient interchangeability between all products forming part of same market insofar as specific use of products is concerned ...' (*Hoffmann-la-Roche v Commission*).

- The relevant market depends on 'cross elasticity of demand' and 'supply'.

3 Examples of the relevant market have included:

- heavy goods vehicle tyres as opposed to tyres generally (*Michelin (NV Nederlandsche Baden-Industrie Michelin) v Commission 322/81*);

- cash register parts (*Hugin Kassaregister AB v Commission 22/78*);

- separate cartons for pasteurised and UHT milk (*Tetra Pak (No 1) T-51/89*).

Geographical market

1 This is 'where the conditions of competition are sufficiently homogenous for the effect of economic power on the undertaking to be evaluated ...' (*United Brands*).

2   In general, the relevant market must be the whole EU, but situations of producers in busy commercial areas are different to those in remote rural areas, even if they enjoy the same market share.

3   So other things will inevitably be taken into account:

- cost, feasibility of transport (*Hilti v Commission* T-30/89);
- pattern/volume of consumption (*Suiker Unie* 40/73).

Temporal market

1   Seasonal factors may be relevant if there is no substitution (*United Brands*).

Calculation of market share

1   No particular market share is required to prove dominance, e.g. a 40% share in *United Brands* was not sufficient on its own – other factors were relevant, e.g. owned own fleet, could control volume of other imports, and highly fragmented rest of market.

2   So other factors must be considered, e.g.:

- competitors' market share was 10% and 16% in *United Brands*;
- superior technological knowledge and sales network in *Michelin*;
- control of production/distribution in *Hoffmann-la-Roche*;
- conduct/performance.

11.3.3 The abuse of the dominant position

1   The abuse, not existence, of a dominant position is prohibited.

2   There is no definition of abuse in the article – though there are some examples.

3   So again it is defined by the ECJ: 'behaviour . . . which is such as to influence the structure of the market where, as a result of the very presence of the undertaking in question, the degree of competition is weakened, and . . . has the effect of hindering the maintenance of the degree of competition . . . or the growth of that competition . . .'.

4   Specific practices identified as abuses in the Article include:

- directly or indirectly imposing unfair purchase or selling prices or other unfair trading conditions, e.g.:

i) price reduction to kill competition (*AKZO v Commission* C-62/86);

ii) differential pricing for different states (*United Brands*);

iii) loyalty rebates (*Hoffmann-la-Roche*);

● limiting production, markets or technical development to the prejudice of consumers (*Magill TV Guide and ITP v Commission* C-241/91 P); can include:

i) exclusive supply agreements (*Hoffman-la-Roche*); and

ii) a refusal to supply (*Sot. Lelos kai Sia EE and Others v GlaxoSmithKline AEVE Farmakeftikon Proionton* C-468/06 to 478/06);

● applying dissimilar conditions to equivalent transactions with other trading parties, thereby placing them at a competitive disadvantage;

● making conclusion of contracts subject to supplementary obligations having no connection with subject of such contracts, e.g. 'tying arrangements' (*Tetra Pak II* (1992)).

11.3.4 Affecting trade between Member States

1   This must be an effect caused by the abuse.

2   The same condition is imposed in Art 101.

3   It is not hard to show.

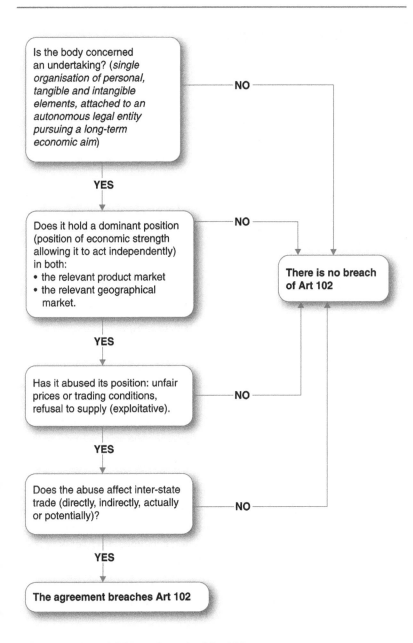

The means of establishing a breach of Art 102

▶ 11.4 Merger control

11.4.1 Merger control under Art 101 and Art 102

1   Prior to 1990 only standard competition law was available to deal with mergers and concentrations.

2   Both needed control because the nature of monopoly power is anti-competitive.

3   So Art 102 might be infringed if a dominant undertaking strengthened its dominance so that the only undertakings to remain in the relevant market are those whose behaviour depends on the dominant one (*Europembellage Corporation and Continental Can v Commission* 6/72).

11.4.2 Merger control originally under Regulation 4064/89

1   Pressure for effective legislation grew by late 1980s.

2   It came in Regulation 4064/89.

3   The purpose of the Regulation was to identify mergers of such a size that they should be controlled by the EU rather than by national authorities which could distort competition.

4   'Concentrations' meeting certain criteria had to be 'notified' to the Commission within one week of the agreement being concluded, if they had a EU dimension:

   ● the undertakings concerned must have a combined world turnover of at least 2,500 million euros; and

   ● turnover in at least three Member States is more than 100 million euros, with turnover of at least two undertakings in three states being more than 25 million euros, and combined turnover of at least two undertakings being more than 100 million euros.

11.4.3 Reform of procedure under Regulation 139/2004

1   Regulation recognises that national authorities are more effective means of control.

2   The test is whether the concentration creates or enhances a dominant position that would lead to effective competition being substantially impeded.

3   Notification is to national authority unless it would involve notification in three or more Member States: then it can be to the Commission and can lead to one of three decisions:

- concentration falls within the scope of the Regulation and gives rise to proceedings because it is potentially incompatible with the requirements of a single market; or

- it falls within the scope of the Regulation but there is no need for proceedings because it is compatible with common market; or

- it falls outside the scope of the Regulation.

4   Art 2(1) requires the Commission to appraise the proposed merger and take account of:

- the need to maintain and develop effective competition – taking into account the structure of the market and the actual competition;

- the market position of the undertaking and their economic and financial power as well as available alternatives, access to suppliers and markets, and any legal barriers, as well as the interests of the consumers;

- even if a concentration of power does not meet thresholds, an EU dimension is possible and there is no breach of Art 102;

- neither Regulation has seemed to present much of a barrier to mergers – however, case law has dealt quite harshly with mergers (*France v Commission* C-68/94 and C-30/95 and *Airtours plc v Commission* T-342/99).

▶ 11.5 Procedural rules

11.5.1 Introduction

1   Powers and procedures were in Regulation 17/62.

2   Now under Regulation 1/2003.

3   The fundamental rule is that infringements of Art 101 and Art 102 are prohibited regardless of any previous rules.

11.5.2 Notification of agreements

1   Under Art 1(1) of the Regulation undertakings themselves must assess whether their agreements breach Art 101 or are exempt under Art 101(3).

2   National authorities can demand that a breach is brought to an end and can order interim measures and also fine.

3   Commission can still investigate and issue Decisions and is still responsible for block exemptions but mainly investigates large price-fixing cartels.

11.5.3 The investigative power of the Commission

1   The Commission can instigate an investigation:

- either on its own initiative; or
- on application of a Member State or interested parties;
- it may only take action after an 'appropriate preliminary investigation';
- and if it decides to act it must notify the applicants.

2   It has extensive power to obtain information from governments, relevant authorities, firms, etc., so it has the right to:

- examine books and other business records;
- take copies or extracts from any of these;
- request on-the-spot oral explanations;
- enter any premises or transport of the undertaking.

11.5.4 Judicial powers of the Commission

1   Undertakings must be allowed a fair hearing.

2   The Commission arranges hearings, having circulated a 'Statement of Objections' – all parties can respond.

11.5.5 Available penalties

1   The Commission can impose two types of financial penalty:

- Fines: from 1,000 to 1,000,000 euros, or a larger amount not over 10% of an undertaking's previous annual turnover. The amount depends on the seriousness and duration of an infringement, subject to 1998 Notice on method of setting fines.
- Periodic payments: incentive-led penalties. The penalty is a specific sum for every day or week the infringement continues, so is an incentive to stop quickly. Payments can vary between 50 and 1,000 euros.

11.5.6 Review by the Court

1   By Regulation 17/62 Commission decisions are reviewable by court.

2   They will take the form of Art 263 or Art 265 actions.

Key Cases Checklist

Meaning of undertaking

***FENIN v Commission* (2003)**
'a single organisation of personal, tangible and intangible elements, attached to an autonomous legal entity and pursuing a long term economic aim'

Competition

Art 101 exemptions
***ACEC v Berliet* (1968)**
Exempt because intermediaries gained, which benefited consumers and there were no restrictions going beyond these positive aims and no threat to competition

Art 101 and restrictive trade practices
Types of prohibited behaviour

***IAZ International Belgium* (1983)**
Applying dissimilar conditions to equivalent transactions

Agreements covered by Art 101

***AEG Telefunken v Commission* (1983)**
Must involve collusive behaviour

***ICI Ltd v Commission (The Dyestuffs Case)* (1972)**
Concerted practices are a form of coordination between enterprises that has not yet reached the point where it is a contract

Affecting trade between Member States

***Belasco v Commission* (1989)**
Must be capable of constituting a threat direct or indirect, actual or potential, on the pattern of trade

Object or effect of preventing/restricting or distorting competition

***Etablissements Consten and Grundig v Commission* (1966)**
The key issue is whether or not competition is affected

***Societe Technique Miniere v Maschinenbau Ulm* (1966)**
But the ECJ try to apply the rules so as not to stifle enterprise and initiative

Art 102 and abuse of a dominant position

***Continental Can Co. v Commission* (1973)**
Dominance is the 'power to behave independently without taking into account their competitors, purchasers or suppliers because of their share of the market or ... availability of technical knowledge, raw materials or capital, they have power to control production or distribution for significant part of products'
***United Brands v Commission* (1978)**
And is measured against the relevant product market and the relevant geographical market
***Hoffmann-la-Roche v Commission* (1979)**
Abuse is where the behaviour of the undertaking 'has the effect of hindering the maintenance of the degree of competition still existing in the market or the growth of that competition'

11.2.1.4   *FENIN v Commission* T-319/99 [2003] ECR II-357

Key Facts

Spanish hospitals and other health care bodies grouped together collectively under the name SNS and purchased supplies from FENIN, a Spanish association made up of most of the firms marketing medical goods and equipment. SNS delayed payment for supplies and FENIN complained that this amounted to an abuse of a dominant position under [Art 102 TFEU], although the claim was rejected.

Key Law

The CFI held that SNS was not an undertaking for the purposes of [Art 101 TFEU] and [Art 102 TFEU]. A purchaser clearly could be classed as an undertaking if the purchases were then used in the context of an economic activity, but SNS was financed by social security contributions and offered a free service to the public.

Key Comment

The established definition of an undertaking is 'a single organisation of personal, tangible and intangible elements, attached to an autonomous legal entity and pursuing a long-term economic aim'. The CFI in *FENIN* refined this definition, identifying that there must be some form of economic activity, however marginal, for an entity to be seen as an 'undertaking' for the purposes of competition law.

11.2.1.4   *Meca-Medina and Majcen v Commission* C519/04P

Key Facts

Two long-distance swimmers had been suspended under the International Olympic Committee's Anti-Doping Code and argued that this infringed competition rules. The Commission rejected their complaint and they appealed its decision to the [General Court], which held that purely sporting rules did not come under EU competition law. On further appeal to the ECJ their action was dismissed as the penalties were not disproportionate.

Key Law

The Court held that sport is subject to EU Law and that the magnitude of penalties imposed by sporting bodies could breach competition law because they may have adverse effects on competition.

11.2.2.1 *AEG Telefunken v Commission* 107/82 [1983] ECR 3151

Key Facts

A company refused to admit a trader to its distribution network and the Commission challenged this as being in breach of [Art 101 TFEU].

Key Law

The Court rejected the argument that there was no agreement between undertakings. It held that this was because the refusal formed part of a system of contracts with the existing distributors.

Key Comment

An agreement between undertakings must always carry with it some form of collusion to distinguish it from purely unilateral acts.

11.2.2.1 *ACF Chemiefarma v Commission (The Quinine Cartel Case)* 41, 44, 45/69 [1970] ECR 661

Key Facts

Firms in France, Germany and the Netherlands agreed to sales quotas on quinine and not to manufacture synthetic quinine. This was challenged by the Commission as in breach of [Art 101 TFEU].

Key Law

The Court held that there was a breach of [Art 101 TFEU]. The agreement had been reached in order to artificially raise the price of the product by limiting its availability and to prevent undertakings outside of the agreement from entering the market. It fell under the second type of prohibited agreement under [Art 101(1) TFEU]: limiting or controlling production, markets, technical development or investment.

11.2.2.3   *ICI Ltd v Commission (The Dyestuffs Case)* 48/69 [1972] ECR 619

Key Facts

The major manufacturers of dyestuff, which represented more than 80% of sales of dyestuff, all raised their prices at exactly the same time. The Commission concluded that there had been a concerted practice and imposed fines on the undertakings. The undertakings challenged this decision and argued that there was no formal agreement, but merely parallel behaviour in an oligopoly (similar to a monopoly but where the majority of a market is controlled by a few undertakings rather than a single body).

Key Law

The ECJ held that it was irrelevant that there was no formal agreement because collusion was identifiable in a series of telexes to subsidiary companies all phrased in the same manner. There was a concerted practice amounting to a breach of [Art 101 TFEU].

Key Judgment

The Court defined concerted practice as 'a form of coordination between enterprises that has not yet reached the point where it is a contract in the true sense of the word, but which, in practice, consciously substitutes co-operation for the risks of competition'. It added that '[it] may . . . arise out of coordination which becomes apparent from the behaviour of the participants' and that, while 'parallel behaviour may not by itself be . . . a concerted practice, it may, however, amount to strong evidence of such a practice if it leads to conditions of competition which do not correspond to the normal conditions of the market'.

Key Link

Cooperatieve Vereeniging 'Suiker Unie' v Commission (The Sugar Cartel Case), 40–48, 50, 54–56, 111, 113, 114/73

[1975] ECR 1663 and see *T-Mobile Netherlands BV and Others v Raad van Bestuur van de Nederlandse Mededingingsautoriteit* C-8/08, where it was held that even a single meeting between companies could amount to a concerted practice.

11.2.2.6

IAZ International Belgium and others v Commission 96/82 [1983] ECR 3369

Key Facts

Under Belgian law only washing machines and dishwashers that conformed to Belgian standards could be connected to the mains water supply. These standards were set in an agreement between the national association of water suppliers and a trade association to which certain major suppliers of washing machines and dishwashers were affiliated. This had the effect of disadvantaging those suppliers who were not affiliated to the trade association, who complained as a result.

Key Law

The ECJ held that this conformed to one of the five types of prohibited anti-competitive behaviour identified in Art 85 (now Art 101 TFEU) since it applied dissimilar conditions to equivalent transactions with other trading parties, placing them at a competitive disadvantage. The other obvious effect was that it provided advantageous conditions to suppliers belonging to the trade association.

11.2.2.6

VBVB and VVVB v Commission 43 & 63/82 [1984] ECR 19

Key Facts

Dutch and Belgian booksellers operated a retail price maintenance agreement which was challenged successfully by the Commission.

Key Law

The Court held that the agreement was one directly or indirectly fixing purchase or selling prices, identified as an anti-competitive practice in [Art 101(1) TFEU]. It covered all books and all publishers and was not capable of exemption under [Art 101(3) TFEU] and so breached [Art 101].

Key Link

Publishers Association v Commission C-360/92P [1995] ECR I-23, where the ECJ held that the 'net book' pricing system in the UK was not in breach of [Art 101 TFEU] since it applied to certain books only and benefited the book trade in the UK and Ireland.

11.2.2.6 *Commission and France v Ladbroke Racing Ltd* C-359 and 379/95P [1998] 4 CMLR 27

Key Facts

French law required that companies which engaged in off-course totalisator betting should be in the control of Pari Mutuel Urbain (PMU). Ladbrokes argued that the agreements between those companies and PMU breached [Art 101 TFEU].

Key Law

The ECJ held that there was no breach since the companies and PMU were operating according to national law. For the agreement to breach [Art 101 TFEU] it would require autonomous behaviour by the undertakings. As a result there could be no breach of [Art 101 TFEU] where national law imposed the agreement on the undertakings.

11.2.2.3 *Belasco v Commission* 246/86 [1989] ECR 2117

Key Facts

Businesses in the Belgian roofing felt industry operated as a cartel and this was challenged as contrary to [Art 101 TFEU].

Key Law

The Court rejected the argument that there was no effect on trade as the agreement was limited to sales in Belgium only. The agreement was capable of affecting trade between Member States as it placed competitors outside of the cartel at a disadvantage. There was a breach of [Art 101 TFEU].

11.2.2.4 *Vereeniging van Cementhandelaren v Commission* 8/72 [1972] ECR 977

Key Facts

An agreement between cement dealers fixed the price of cement throughout the Netherlands. It was challenged by the Commission as being in breach of [Art 101 TFEU].

Key Law

The Court held that the agreement was capable of affecting trade between Member States, even though the agreement was limited to the Netherlands, because it would strengthen existing divisions in the market and make penetration from other Member States more difficult, thereby protecting the domestic industry.

11.2.2.2 *Etablissements Consten and Grundig v Commission* 56 & 58/64 [1966] ECR 299

Key Facts

Under an exclusive dealership agreement Consten was appointed sole distributor of Grundig's electrical goods in France in return for accepting that it would not import or export Grundig's products in any other EU country. Another company, UNEF, then sold Grundig's goods in France in breach of Consten's exclusive rights. Consten complained to the Commission and UNEF counterclaimed that the dealership was a breach of [Art 101 TFEU]. The Commission issued a decision on this basis. Consten and Grundig argued that the agreement was for the purpose of stream-lining distribution of Grundig's products in France, where Grundig had competition from other manufacturers, and was not an interference with trade.

Key Law

The ECJ held that both vertical agreements (within the chain of production and distribution) and horizontal agreements (between competitors) were covered by [Art 101 TFEU]. The exclusive dealership did breach [Art 101 TFEU] since it might affect trade between Member States by putting other businesses at a competitive disadvantage. It was irrelevant whether trade had been affected; it was sufficient that the agreement was intended to stifle competition.

11.2.2.2   *Societe Technique Miniere v Maschinenbau Ulm (the STM case) 56/65 [1966] ECR 337*

Key Facts

Under an exclusive supply agreement STM was given sole rights to sell Maschinenbau's heavy earth-moving equipment in France. In contrast to *Consten & Grundig*, there was no agreement for exclusive use of the trademark, nor was there a ban on parallel imports or exports. The question for the ECJ was whether the agreement was capable of preventing, distorting or restricting competition.

Key Law

The Court held that since the agreement was clearly made only because it was necessary to enable a firm penetration of the goods in a new market, and was therefore aimed purely at business efficiency, it did not breach [Art 101 TFEU].

Key Comment

The case is important because the Court also listed factors to be taken into account in deciding whether an agreement is capable of restricting, preventing or distorting competition:

- the nature and quantity of the product;
- the position and size of the undertakings in the market;
- the relationship with other agreements;
- the extent of the agreement;
- the link to parallel imports or exports.

11.2.2.2

Franz Volk v Etablissements Vervaecke Sprl 5/69 [1969] ECR 295

Key Facts

In an agreement between a Dutch electrical goods distributor (Vervaecke) and a German washing machine manufacturer (Volk), the Dutch firm gained exclusive distribution rights for the German company's washing machines in Belgium and Luxembourg. In return it agreed to a ban on parallel imports of Volk's products by third parties, a total protection for the German company.

Key Law

The ECJ accepted that, since Volk produced only between 0.2% and 0.5% of washing machines in Germany and sold considerably fewer in Belgium and Luxembourg, the agreement could not be said to have any real effect on competition, the *de minimis* principle applied and there was no breach of [Art 101 TFEU].

Key Comment

This is now covered by the Commission Notice on Agreements of Minor Importance 2001 C368/13 with limits of total market share of 10% for horizontal agreements and 15% for vertical agreements.

11.2.3.4

Re Vacuum Interrupters (Decision 77/160) [1977] 1 CMLR D67

Key Facts

Different manufacturers of switchgear engaged in a joint venture for the development of vacuum interrupters and applied to the Commission for exemption under [Art 101(3) TFEU].

Key Law

The Commission issued a decision exempting the agreement since it met all four requirements of [Art 101(3) TFEU]. It improved production and promoted technical progress since it made research possible. It would benefit consumers, did not impose unnecessary restrictions, and would not eliminate competition since the market stretched well beyond the EU and the undertakings faced significant competition from both the USA and Japan.

11.2.3.4 — *ACEC v Berliet* (Decision 68/39) [1968] CMLR D35

Key Facts

Two French manufacturers agreed jointly on the production of a prototype bus and applied for exemption under [Art 101(3) TFEU].

Key Law

The Commission granted exemption since a benefit was gained by intermediaries in the distribution network which would ultimately benefit consumers. There were no restrictions going beyond these positive aims and no threat to competition.

11.3.1.3 — *Italian Flat Glass Cartel* (Decision 89/93) [1992] 5 CMLR 120

Key Facts

A group of undertakings enjoyed a share of between 79% and 95% of the market for production of 'flat glass' and were challenged when they engaged in concerted price fixing.

Key Law

The Commission accepted that this was a dominant position and that Art [Art 102 TFEU] could be invoked.

11.3.2.2 — *Continental Can Co. v Commission* 6/72 [1973] ECR 215

Key Facts

Continental Can, a US multi-national, through its European subsidiary, Europemballage, had an 86% share in

Schmalbach, another company. Schmalbach had a dominant position in Germany in the market for tins for meat and
fish products and for metal lids for glass containers.
Europemballage then proposed a takeover of a Dutch
packaging firm, Thomassen, and this was challenged as
being a breach of [Art 102 TFEU]. The Commission held
that it was an elimination of potential competition and
reduced consumer choice, and so was an abuse of a dominant position.

Key Law

The ECJ overturned the Commission's Decision on the
ground that the Commission had failed to identify the relevant product market and therefore had not in fact proved
dominance.

Key Judgment

*The Court defined dominance as 'power to behave inde-
pendently without taking into account their competitors,
purchasers or suppliers because of their share of the market
or . . . availability of technical knowledge, raw materials or
capital, they have power to control production or distribution for significant part of products'.*

11.3.2.2 | ### *United Brands v Commission* 27/76 [1978] ECR 207

Key Facts

United Brands was one of the largest producers of bananas
in the world, handling 40% of [EU] trade at the time. It was
charging different prices in different Member States for the
same goods. When this was challenged as being both in
breach of [Art 101 TFEU] and an abuse of its dominant
position under [Art 102 TFEU], United Brands argued that
the relevant product market was fresh fruit, in which case it
would have only a very small market share and dominance
would not be an issue. The Commission argued, and it was
accepted, that there was in fact a separate product market
for bananas. This was because it was shown that bananas
had a very specific market, usually being consumed by the
sick, the aged and the young. They could not therefore
be considered merely as a part of a much more general
market.

Key Law

The ECJ held that there was a breach of [Art 102 TFEU] and considered again the definition of dominance. This involved considering both the relevant product market and the relevant geographical market and market share. The market share for bananas enjoyed by the company in Europe was between 40% and 45%, which was held to be a dominant position. However, as the ECJ noted, where the market share is less than 50% other factors must be considered, including the share of the nearest competitors. The two closest competitors in trade of bananas held 16% and 10% of the market.

Key Judgment

The ECJ, building on its definition in Continental Can, identified that dominance is 'a position of economic strength . . . which enables it to prevent competition being maintained on the relevant market by giving it the power to behave to an appreciable effect independently of its competitors, and ultimately its consumers'.

Key Comment

The case identifies that market share alone is not conclusive evidence of dominance. United Brands owned its own fleet and could control the volume of other imports. The rest of the market was also highly fragmented. There was reasonably healthy competition in the relevant market but not enough to prevent United Brands being able to act independently of its competitors.

11.3.2.2 *Hoffmann-la-Roche v Commission* 85/76 [1979] ECR 461

Key Facts

Hoffman La Roche offered loyalty rebates to purchasers of its vitamins and this was challenged as being in breach of [Art 102 TFEU]. The company enjoyed a market share in the relevant product amounting to more than 80%.

Key Law

The ECJ held that there was an obvious position of dominance in view of market share and also an obvious disadvantage to their competitors amounting to an abuse, so there was a breach. The Court also identified that the relevant product market includes not only the product itself but other products that could be substituted for it.

Key Judgment

On dominance the Court held 'such a position does not preclude some competition but enables [it] . . . if not to determine, at least to have an appreciable effect on the conditions in which that competition will develop, and in any case to act largely in disregard of it'. It also defined abuse as 'an objective concept relating to the behaviour of an undertaking which is such as to influence the structure of the market where, as a result of the very presence of the undertaking in question, the degree of competition is weakened, and which, through recourse to methods different from those which conditions normal competition in products or services on the basis of the transactions of commercial operators, has the effect of hindering the maintenance of the degree of competition still existing in the market or the growth of that competition'.

11.3.2.3   *NV Nederlandsche Baden-Indutrie Michelin v Commission* 322/81 [1983] ECR 3461

Key Facts

The company supplied tyres for heavy earth-moving vehicles and offered bonuses to dealers for marketing effort but with no clear basis for calculation. The Commission challenged this as being an abuse of a dominant position.

Key Law

The Court accepted that there was a distinct product market since there was nothing to link the product to tyres in general. It also accepted that the Netherlands could be the relevant geographical market because of the effect on competition since, by contrast to competitors, the company possessed not only advanced technology but had a history of supplying such specialist products.

11.3.2.3   *Hugin Kassaregister AB v Commission* 22/78
[1979] ECR 1869

Key Facts

A Swedish firm manufacturing cash registers refused to
supply spare parts to an English company which serviced
and repaired such machines only in the UK. The Commission
argued that this breached [Art 102 TFEU].

Key Law

The Court accepted that there was a discrete relevant
product market for the goods. However, it held that the
abuse did not affect trade between Member States since it
did not prevent the English company from operating in other
Member States, and Sweden was not at the time in the EU.

11.3.2.3   *Tetra Pak International v Commission (No 2)*
T-83/91 [1994] ECR II-755

Key Facts

The firm invented a process for filling cartons that would
prolong the shelf life of the foodstuff to six months. It then
refused to sell the machines for the process unless
customers also bought the cartons (tetra paks) from its
subsidiary company.

Key Law

The Court accepted that there was no interchangeability of
product so that the packaging was a relevant product
market. It also held that the additional requirement in the
contract was an abuse. It was making the completion of
contracts subject to supplementary obligations that had no
connection with the main contract.

11.3.2.3   *Hilti v Commission* T-30/89 [1990]
ECR II-163

Key Facts

A firm was the dominant supplier of nail cartridges for its
nail guns and was challenged by the Commission on the

conditions it imposed. The Commission rejected the argument that there was cross-elasticity of supply between nail guns and power drills.

Key Law

The Court, in deciding that there was a breach of [Art 102 TFEU], accepted that the nail guns were a discrete product market and also that the relevant geographical market was the whole of the EU because of the ease and small cost of transporting the nail cartridges.

11.3.3.4   *AKZO v Commission* C-62/86 [1986] ECR 1503

Key Facts

A company that enjoyed a dominant position in the benzole peroxide market cut its prices over a long period of time. It did so in order to put a small British competitor out of business.

Key Law

The Court held that using price reductions to prevent competition did amount to an abuse. Any instance of directly or indirectly imposing unfair purchase or selling prices would amount to abuse.

11.3.3.4   *Magill TV Guide & ITP v Commission* C-241/91 P [1995] ECR I-743

Key Facts

Television companies which were the sole source of TV listings refused to supply the information to companies producing weekly listings for all channels, and the practice was challenged.

Key Law

The Court held that the refusal was only to protect the company's own publications. There was a market for the product and the refusal therefore was to the prejudice of consumers and amounted to an abuse and a breach of [Art 102 TFEU].

Equal pay:

- By Art 157 'men and women shall receive equal pay for equal work'.
- Art 157 is directly effective (*Defrenne v SABENA*).
- Comparator need not be in contemporary empoyment (*Macarthys v Smith*).
- Wide definition of 'pay' – ordinary basic or minimum wage or salary or any other consideration, whether in cash or in kind, received directly or indirectly – so could include concessionary travel (*Garland v BREL*) and contracted out pension (*Barber v Guardian Royal Assurance Group*) etc.
- Supplemented and explained in Directive 2006/54, which includes an action for work of equal value (*Hayward v Cammell Laird Shipbuilders*).
- But can only receive equal pay, even if work shown to be of superior value (*Murphy v An Bord Telecom Eireann*).
- Possible to pay differential pay rates to part-timers provided there is an 'objective justification' (*Bilka-Kaufhaus*) if:
    - i) corresponds to genuine need of enterprise;
    - ii) suitable for obtaining objective pursued by the enterprise;
    - iii) necessary for that purpose.

Equal access:

- Found in Directive 2006/54 – 'in access to employment, including promotion and to vocational training and … working conditions there shall be equal treatment for men and women'.
- Derogation permitted for activities where sex is a determining factor (*Johnston v RUC*) or for protection of women.
- But positive discrimination not allowed (*Kalanke v Frei Hausestadt Bremen*).
- Has been used in pregnancy on dismissal (*Webb v EMO (Air Cargo)*) or employment denied (*Dekker v Stichting*).
- Has been used for unequal retirement ages (*Marshall v Southampton AHA*).
- Usual problems associated with direct effect of directives, but may be indirectly effective under the *Von Colson* principle (*Beets-Proper v F. Van Lanschot Bankiers NV*).

DISCRIMINATION LAW

Social security:

- Directive 79/7 extends equal access principle to social security.
- Applies to statutory schemes protecting against sickness, invalidity, old age, accidents at work, occupational diseases, and unemployment.
- Can exclude: deciding pensionable age, benefits for people who have brought up children, wives' derived invalidity or old age benefits, increases granted to dependent wife.

New developments:

Two directives of 2000 now in force:
- one on race;
- one more general includes, e.g. sexual orientation, disability, religion and belief.

Self-employment

- Found in Directive 86/613.
- Applies to all persons pursuing a gainful activity for their own account.
- Ensures Member States eliminate discrimination.

▶ 12.1 Introduction

1 Equality is a fundamental principle of EU law, and is used as one of the general principles of law, so all measures are ultimately subject to it.

2 Sexual equality was seen as a natural extension of the principle of national equality.

3 Art 157, then, was one of the first substantive provisions created to ensure that two distinct objectives are achieved:

   ● an economic objective – the elimination of unfair advantages which would distort free competition;

   ● a social objective – the general improvement of living and working conditions throughout the EU.

4 Art 157 stated and simply requires that 'Member States shall ensure that . . . men and women receive equal pay for equal work . . .'.

5 It was later supplemented by many Directives:

   ● 75/117 – the Equal Pay Directive;

   ● 76/207 – the Equal Treatment Directive;

   ● 79/7 – the Equal Treatment in Social Security Directive;

   ● 86/378 – the Equal Treatment in Occupational Pension Schemes Directive;

   ● 86/613 – Equal Treatment in Self-employment Directive. Now Directive 2006/54, the 'Recast Directive' repeals and replaces all but the last of these.

6 Case law of the ECJ (with the exception of one aspect of *Defrenne v SABENA*) has been consistent in preventing national interests from subverting the general principle:

   ● most of the case law in Art 267 references has involved rectifying the narrow interpretations by national courts;

   ● it has been instrumental in developing the law on, e.g., fair treatment of pregnant women and other areas.

7 The Commission has also been active, e.g. developing law on sexual harassment – defined in their Code of Practice.

8 Art 157 is directly effective (*Defrenne v SABENA (No 2) 43/75*):

   ● It is effective horizontally and vertically because it is a Treaty article and satisfies all of the *Reyner* test.

   ● Unfortunately, national demands by the UK and Ireland led to it being only prospectively directly effective.

9   Subsequently, many of the Directives have also been held to be directly effective (but only vertically because Directives fail the *Reyner* test), leading to anomalies and so judicial activism by the ECJ (see *Marshall v Southampton and S.W. Hampshire AHA* and also *Duke v Reliance GEC*).

▶ 12.2 Art 157 and equal pay

12.2.1 The meaning of pay

1   The ECJ has had none of the problems encountered by, for example, English courts in establishing the existence of a comparator of the opposite sex (*Macarthys v Smith* 129/79).

2   Most actions in the ECJ have focused on the meaning of pay:

- defined in Art 157 as 'the ordinary basic or minimum wage or salary or any other consideration, whether in cash or in kind, which the worker receives directly or indirectly, in respect of his employment from his employer';

- so pay has a much broader meaning in Art 157 than in the Equal Pay Act, and interpretation is purposive.

3   Pay has been held to include:

- perks, e.g. concessionary rail fares for retired railway workers (*Garland v BREL* 12/81) and supplementary payments into an occupational pension scheme (*Worringham and Humphries v Lloyds Bank Ltd* 69/80);

- bonuses (*Brunnhofer* C-381/99);

- sick pay (*Rinner-Kuhn v FWW Spezial Gebaudereinigung GmbH and Co. KG* 171/88);

- paid leave for training (*Arbeiterwohlifahrt der Stadt Berlin v Botel*);

- contractual non-contributory occupational pension schemes, supplementing state schemes, denied to part-timers (*Bilka-Kaufhaus v Karen Weber von Harz* 170/84);

- unequal retirement ages (*Marshall v Southampton and South West Hampshire AHA (Teaching) (No 1)* 152/84);

- redundancy payments (*R v Secretary of State for Employment ex parte Equal Opportunities Commission* (1994) (HL));

- EAT has suggested it may include compensation for unfair dismissal (*Mediguard Services Ltd v Thame* (1994)) also – in *R v Secretary of State for Employment ex parte Seymour-Smith and*

Perez [1999] ECR 1-623 – the Court of Justice stated that such an award would amount to a form of deferred pay;

- 'contracted out' pension schemes which depend for operation on different retirement ages, as in *Barber v Guardian Royal Assurance Group 262/88*. The case is also important in identifying that Art 157 is infringed if pension rights are deferred in a person made compulsorily redundant to retirement age (if different to person of opposite sex), so applies *Marshall* logic to contracted out schemes, but had prospective direct effect like *Defrenne*.

4　Pension rights are also covered in the subsequent directives, but ECJ rulings are important in UK because death and retirement was not covered by English law in the Equal Pay Act.

5　When considering inequality the ECJ will have regard to every different aspect of pay separately and compare on each level (*Handels-og Kontorfunktionaerenes Forbund v Dansk Arbejdsgiverforening for Danfoss 109/88*).

6　This contrasts sharply with the original attitude of the English courts to take a 'whole contract' view (*Hayward v Cammell Laird Shipbuilders* (1986)).

7　Contrary to the original UK interpretation of the Equal Pay Act, the ECJ has held that the comparator need not be in contemporaneous employment (*Macarthys v Smith 129/79*), which is now accepted in English law (*Diocese of Hallam Trustees v Connaughton* (1996)).

8　But cannot involve the same work but for a different employer (*Lawrence and others C-320/00*).

9　It may be possible to pay differential pay rates to part-timers and justify discrimination provided there is an 'objective justification' (*Bilka-Kaufhaus*), which it will be if it:

- corresponds to a genuine need of the enterprise;
- is suitable for obtaining the objective pursued by the enterprise;
- is necessary for that purpose.

▶ 12.3 Equal Pay and Directive 2006/54

12.3.1 Equal pay for the same work and for work of equal value

1　Art 119 (now Art 157 TFEU) gave a limited description of pay.

2　This was remedied in Directive 75/117 (now replaced by Directive 2006/54, the Recast Directive). This identified that equal pay should mean 'for same work or for work to which equal value is attributed, the elimination of all discrimination on grounds of sex and regards to all aspects and conditions of remuneration'.

3   'Same work' does not have to be identical nor need it involve contemporaneous employment (*Macarthys v Smith* 129/79).

4   But discrimination only exists where the differential term is based on sex alone (*Jenkins v Kingsgate Clothing Ltd* 96/80).

5   Discrimination might be direct (*Dekker v Stichting Vormingscentrum Voor Jong Volwassenen* C-177/88) or indirect (*Jenkins v Kingsgate Clothing*), e.g. by giving different rates to part-timers.

6   To bring an 'equal value claim' a woman must show that her job, though different to the man's, is equal in the demands made on her in terms of effort, skill, decision making, etc. and thus of equal value to the employer.

● Proving a claim will depend on the result of a job evaluation study instigated as a result of the claim.

● ECJ guidelines on such schemes are in *Rummler v Dato-Druck GmbH 237/85*. The scheme could be acceptable if:

i)   the system as a whole precluded discrimination on grounds of sex;

ii) the criteria employed were objectively justified, which they would be if they:

a)   are appropriate to tasks to be carried out; and

b)   correspond with genuine need of undertaking.

● *Danfoss* extended the criteria to include flexibility and seniority.

● Directive 2006/54 (the Recast Directive) requires Member States to ensure that provisions of collective agreements, wage scales, wage agreements, or individual contracts of employment contrary to the principle of equality are invalidated. In *Cadman* C-17/05 [2006] the Court of Justice identified that incremental pay scales could be justified on the basis of the extra experience offered by the worker except 'where the worker provides evidence capable of giving rise to serious doubts as to whether recourse to the criterion of length of service is, in the circumstances, appropriate'.

● It is also the Member State's responsibility to ensure that citizens have the means to bring such a claim – so the UK was taken to the ECJ originally under [Art 258 TFEU] infringement proceedings in *Commission v UK* 61/81 (leading to the Equal Pay (Amendment) Act 1983, the first claim being *Hayward v Camel Laird Shipbuilders* (1986)), as was Luxembourg in *Commission v Luxembourg* 58/81.

- It was shown that provisions in UK law in the Employment Protection Consolidation Act 1978 (now Employment Rights Act 1996) on part-time workers offend EC (now EU) law (*R v Secretary of State for Employment, ex parte Equal Opportunities Commission* (1994)).

- The old two-year qualifying period for unfair dismissal was also challenged (*R v Secretary of State for Employment, ex parte Seymour-Smith* (1997)).

- One major anomaly of the 'equal value claim' is that the woman can only receive equal pay, even if her work is shown to be of superior value (*Murphy v An Bord Telecom Eireann* 157/86).

- In some situations a claim could be brought under the Directive or Art 157, in which case the latter is preferable because of direct effect implications.

▶ 12.4 Equal treatment

1   This was introduced under Art 308 rather than Art 119 [Art 157 TFEU]: 'If action by the [EU] is . . . necessary to attain . . . one of the objectives . . . and this Treaty has not provided the necessary powers, the Council shall . . . take the appropriate measures . . .'

2   Directive 2006/54 provides for equal treatment on grounds of sex in pay, conditions of employment, including access to and termination of employment, and in occupational social security systems – this necessarily includes provision against discrimination of transsexuals (*KB v National Health Service Pensions Agency* C-117/01 [2004]).

3   The Directive defines discrimination:

- under Art 2(1)(a) (which deals with sex discrimination) 'direct discrimination' occurs where 'one person is treated less favourably on grounds of sex than another is, has been or would be treated in a comparable situation';

- under Art 2(1)(b) indirect 'discrimination' occurs where 'an apparently neutral provision, criterion or practice would put persons of one sex at a particular disadvantage compared with persons of the other sex, unless that provision, criterion or practice is objectively justified by a legitimate aim, and the means of achieving that aim are appropriate and necessary';

- under Art 2(1)(d) sexual harrassment occurs 'where any form of unwanted verbal, non-verbal or physical conduct of a sexual nature occurs, with the purpose or effect of violating the dignity of a person, in particular when creating an intimidating, hostile, degrading, humiliating or offensive environment'.

4 Derogation is permitted under Art 14(2) for 'activities for which the sex of the worker constitutes a genuine and determining occupational requirement, provided that its objective is legitimate and the requirement is proportionate' (*Johnston v Chief Constable of the Royal Ulster Constabulary* 222/84), e.g. specialist army combat units (*Sirdar v Secretary of State for Defence* C-273/97).

- It is for national courts to determine how national legislation is interpreted, but:
  - i) derogation can only apply to specific duties, not activities in general;
  - ii) the situation must be periodically reviewed to ensure it is still justified;
  - iii) the principle of proportionality must apply;
  - iv) the Recast Directive also introduces a reverse burden of proof;
- derogation was also possible under the original Equal Treatment Directive for 'provisions concerning the protection of women, particularly as regards pregnancy and maternity . . .', but the same provision will not protect men (*Hofman v Barmer Ersatzkasse* 184/83);
- and by Art 157(4) TFEU Member States are able to engage in positive discrimination to prevent unequal treatment of women; this is described in Art 3 of the Directive as adopting measures that allow women to compete on a level playing field, but not to the extent of using quotas (*Kalanke v Frei Hausestadt Bremen* C-450/93).

5 The original ETD also had particular use in pregnancy:

- where access to employment is denied (*Dekker v Stichting* C-177/88);
- or on dismissal during maternity leave (*Hertz* 179/88);
- or for any dismissal purely on the grounds of pregnancy (*Webb v EMO Air Cargo* C-2/93).

6 The Equal Treatment Directive has also been useful in relation to unequal retirement ages (*Marshall* – although retirement ages generally come under Directive 79/7 (*Burton v British Railways Board* 19/81)).

7 It was also useful in relation to the calculation of pensionable age for redundancy (*Barber v Guardian Royal Exchange* C-262/88).

8 There are the usual problems associated with direct effect of Directives, but may be indirectly effective under the *Von Colson* principle (*Beets-Proper v F. Van Lanschot Bankiers NV* 262/84).

▶ 12.5 Directive 79/7 and equal treatment in matters of social security

1   This extended the basic principle of equal treatment to social security matters:

- by Art 2 it applies to the working population: 'self-employed persons, workers and self-employed persons whose activity is interrupted by illness, accident, or involuntary unemployment and persons seeking employment ... retired or invalided workers and self-employed persons ...';

- and it has been interpreted broadly (*Drake v Chief Adjudication Officer* 150/85 on carers and see also *Richards* C-423/04 [2006]).

2   Under Art 3 the principles apply to:

- statutory schemes giving protection against sickness, invalidity, old age, accidents at work, occupational diseases, and unemployment;

- social assistance in so far as it is intended to supplement or replace the statutory schemes.

3   Under Art 4 there will be no discrimination in:

- the scope of the schemes and conditions of access to them;

- obligation to contribute and calculation of contributions;

- calculation of benefits including cover of benefits;

- duration of the benefit.

4   So it can apply, for example, to invalidity payment to part-time workers (*Ruzius-Wilbrink v Bestuur van de Bedrifsvereniging voor Overheidsdiensten* 102/88).

5   Art 7 allows Member States to exclude certain matters:

- determination of pensionable age;

- benefits for people who have brought up children;

- wives' derived invalidity or old-age benefits;

- increases granted to a dependent wife.

6   But some aspects would come under it, e.g. *Marshall, Burton*, and it would not apply to, for example, exemption from prescription charges based on differential pensionable age (*R v Secretary of State for Health, ex parte Richardson* C-137/94).

▶ ## 12.6 Directive 86/613 and equal treatment in self-employment

1   This extends the principle of equal treatment to self-employment.

2   Art 2 applies to 'all persons pursuing a gainful activity for their own account – including farmers and members of the liberal professions . . . and spouses not being employees or partners where they habitually participate in activities of self-employed worker and perform same tasks or ancillary tasks . . .'.

3   So Member States must ensure that all discrimination is eliminated in:

● establishment, equipment, extension or launching of any business (Art 4);

● formation of companies between spouses (Art 5);

● access to social security schemes (Art 6).

▶ ## 12.7 The wider anti-discrimination agenda

1   Art 157 TFEU is now a base for introducing directives based on equality.

2   The original Treaty provision was limited to sexual equality, but a separate clause in Art 13 allowed the Commission to take appropriate action to combat discrimination based on 'sex, racial or ethnic origin, religion or belief, disability, age, or sexual orientation'.

3   Two new Directives are now in force:

● the first, the Race Directive 2000/43, is on race discrimination in employment (and limited specific non-employment areas) which broadens the UK meaning of indirect discrimination;

● the second, the Framework Directive 2000/78, applies to employment only on discrimination on age, sexual orientation, disability, religion and belief;

● these have been implemented in UK law initially by statutory instrument but now under the Equality Act 2010.

4   Both Directives share the principle of equal treatment and the core areas of prohibited discrimination now found in the Recast Directive and referrals have already occurred:

● on age discrimination (*Palacios de la Villa* C-411/05 [2007] and *Wolf* C-229/08 [2010]; and *Seda Kucukdeveci v Swedex GmbH & Co KG* C-555/07);

● on race discrimination (*Feryn* C-54/07) [2008]);

- on sexual orientation *Maruko* C-267/06 [2008]);
- on disability (*Chacón Navas* C-13/05 [2006]).

5   More directives and soft law are due in the Social Policy Agenda.

Key Cases Checklist

Equal pay

***Defrenne v SABENA* (1976)**
Art 157 TFEU is directly effective
***Bilka-Kaufhaus v Karen Weber Von Harz* (1986)**
Can only have differential pay rates if there is an 'objective justification':
- corresponds to genuine need of enterprise
- suitable for obtaining objective pursued by the enterprise
- necessary for that purpose

***Barber v Guardian Royal Assurance Group* (1990)**
Pay is defined broadly in Art 157 and includes any benefit an employee obtains by reason of the relationship with the employer
***Rummler v Dato-Druck GmbH* (1986)**
For claims of equal pay for work of equal value job evaluation schemes must not apply different criteria to men and women
***Murphy v An Bord Telecom Eireann* (1988)**
Only equal pay can be awarded by the court even if work shown to be of superior value

Equal treatment

***Johnston v RUC* (1987)**
Derogation is permitted for activities where sex is a determining factor or for the protection of women
***Kalanke v Frei Hausestadt Bremen* (1995)**
But positive discrimination is not allowed
***Webb v EMO (Air Cargo)* (1992)**
Dismissal on grounds of pregnancy is discriminatory and a breach of Directive 2006/57
***Dekker v Stichting* (1990)**
As is refusal to employ on the same grounds
***Marshall v Southampton AHA* (1986)**
As is applying unequal retirement ages

Discrimination

The new anti-discrimination agenda

***Prais v The Council* (1976)**
Freedom of religion was accepted as an essential principle of EC (now EU) law and is now covered by the 'Framework Directive'
***P v S* (1996)**
And unequal treatment of transsexuals has been held to be based on their sex and is therefore discriminatory and in breach of EU law

12.1.8 *Defrenne v SABENA (No 2)* 43/75 [1976] ECR 455

Key Facts

Defrenne was employed as an air stewardess with the Belgian airline SABENA and was paid significantly less than male cabin crew. She was unable to claim equal pay under Belgian law as there was no legislation on equal pay. She tried to bring an action under [Art 157 TFEU] and the Belgian authorities argued that the Art only affected the state and gave no rights to individuals.

Key Law

The Court held that, since the Article complied with all of the *Van Gend en Loos* criteria for direct effect, in the absence of appropriate national law she could use the Article as the basis of her claim for equal pay. It also identified that the Article was both vertically and horizontally directly effective so could be used against private individuals as well as the state.

Key Judgment

The Court stated that the prohibition on discrimination in pay 'applies not only to the actions of public authorities but also extends to all agreements which are intended to regulate paid labour collectively, as well as to contracts between individuals'.

Key Problem

Unfortunately, following representations from the UK and Ireland, the Article was held to be only prospectively, not retrospectively directly effective, meaning that many women lost out on potential and justifiable claims in those countries.

12.2.1.1 *Macarthys Ltd v Smith* 129/79 [1980] ECR 1275

Key Facts

A stockroom manageress discovered that her male predecessor had received significantly higher wages for the job.

She claimed equal pay and the English court held that there was no claim as there was no contemporaneous male in the same employment.

Key Law

The ECJ held that comparison could be made with any male doing the same work for the same or an associated employer and there did not have to be contemporaneous employment. What could not be done was to use a hypothetical male comparator, but this was not the case here. In his reasoned opinion, the Advocate-General also suggested that 'equal work' could include jobs with a high degree of similarity even if they were not exactly the same.

12.2.1.1   *Allonby v Accrington and Rossendale College* C-256/01 [2004] 1 CMLR 35

Key Facts

The college dismissed all of its part-time lecturers, two-thirds of whom were women, before rehiring them through an agency. They were then paid less and lost other benefits, including pension rights. One of the women brought an action under [Art 157 TFEU], naming one of the male full-timers as a comparator.

Key Law

The Court held that there was no possible action under [Art 157 TFEU] as the employers were now different rather than the same.

Key Link

Lawrence and Others v North Yorkshire County Council C-320/00 [2002] ECR I-7325, where the same applied to cleaners working for tendered private companies.

12.2.1.3   *Garland v BREL* 12/81 [1982] ECR 359

Key Facts

The claimant challenged the policy of her employer to offer concessionary travel rates to former male employees and their families on retirement but not to former female employees.

Key Law

The ECJ held that the concession should be available on a non-discriminatory basis irrespective of the fact that it was not founded in contractual entitlement but was a mere perk.

Key Comment

Art 157(2) defines pay in broad terms as the 'ordinary basic or minimum wage or salary or any other consideration, whether in cash or in kind, which the worker receives directly or indirectly, in respect of his employment'. The definition is much broader than that in English employment law. Nevertheless, the Court was still prepared to give a generous interpretation of this broad definition.

12.2.1.3 *Worringham & Humphries v Lloyds Bank Ltd* 69/80 [1981] ECR 767

Key Facts

The bank made supplementary payments to male employees under the age of 25 towards contributions to an occupational pension scheme. It did not make the same concession towards female employees of the same age and was challenged by female employees as being in breach of [Art 157 TFEU].

Key Law

The Court of Justice held that sums which are included within the calculation of an employee's gross salary which are used to directly determine the calculation of other benefits such as redundancy payment, family credit etc. constitute pay for the purposes of [Art 157 TFEU]. Since the subsidy was denied to women under the age of 25 in the context of the case this amounted to a clear breach of [Art 157 TFEU].

Key Comment

[Art 157 TFEU] was preferred in the case to Directive 75/117 (now replaced by Directive 2006/54, the Recast Directive) since there was no problem in establishing the direct effect of a Treaty Article in contrast to the problems that occur in relation to Directives when the claim is against a private individual.

12.2.1.3

Rinner-Kuhn v FWW Spezial Gebaudereinigung GmbH & Co KG 171/88 [1989] ECR 2743

Key Facts

A part-time office cleaner was denied sick pay by her employers. She successfully challenged German legislation that permitted employers to exclude employees working under ten hours per week from sick pay entitlement.

Key Law

The ECJ held that continued payment of employees during periods of sickness absence fell within the definition of pay in Art 119(2). On this basis any legislation allowing employers to discriminate globally against a particular group of employees, part-timers, who were shown to be predominantly female, was in clear breach of [Art 157 TFEU].

12.2.1.3

Bilka-Kaufhaus v Karen Weber von Harz 170/84 [1986] ECR 1607

Key Facts

Harz was employed by a large department store for ten years full time and then part time. Only 10% of male employees worked part time in contrast to 27.7% of women. Harz complained about the occupational pension scheme, only available to employees who had worked full time for 15 of the last 20 years, and from which she was excluded. The store accepted that it deliberately discriminated against part-time work but claimed this was for the genuine need of the business to discourage part-time work because part-timers were less likely to be prepared to work late afternoons and Saturdays.

Key Law

The ECJ held that this could amount to indirect discrimination. Although the provision was neutral it could have a greater impact on women employees because of the ratio of part-time male and female employees. The Court also held that occupational pension schemes could be classed as pay for the purposes of [Art 157 TFEU].

Key Comment

The Court left it to national courts to decide whether there is a real need to apply different rules for part-timers, identifying that there must be an objective justification for doing so. It also set the criteria for determining whether there is an objective justification:

● the measure must correspond to a genuine need of the business;

● it must be suitable for obtaining the objective;

● it must be necessary for that purpose.

In the event the national court decided that there was no objective justification for the discrimination.

12.2.1.3   *R v Secretary of State for Employment, ex p Seymour-Smith and Perez* C-167/97 [1999] ECR I-623

Key Facts

Two women complained that the then two-year qualifying period in English law for unfair dismissal rights unfairly discriminated against women because at any given time more women would fall within that period than men because of career breaks for child rearing.

Key Law

The ECJ held that awards of compensation for unfair dismissal did count as pay for the purposes of [Art 157 TFEU]. The Court considered that such compensation is a form of deferred pay which the worker is entitled to as a result of her employment, and that the sum in effect represented what the worker should have earned if the employer had not unlawfully terminated the employment relationship. The Court added that it was for the Member State to determine whether in fact there had been discrimination by deciding whether a significant number of women were indeed affected.

Key Judgment

The Court stated that 'In order to establish whether a measure adopted by a Member State has disparate effect as between men and women to such a degree as to amount to indirect discrimination . . . the national court must verify whether the statistics available indicate that a considerably smaller percentage of women than men is able to fulfil the requirement'.

12.2.1.3

Barber v Guardian Royal Assurance Group 262/88 [1990] ECR I-8889

Key Facts

Barber was made redundant at the age of 52 and, while he was paid the statutory redundancy payment by his employer, the employer would not pay him an early retirement pension under the contracted out scheme because this was only available to men over the age of 55 when made redundant. In contrast women in similar circumstances were eligible for the early pension scheme at age 50. Barber challenged the rule as being in breach of [Art 157 TFEU].

Key Law

The ECJ held that money paid out under such schemes was indeed pay for the purposes of [Art 157 TFEU] and so there was an unjustified breach of the Article in Barber's case. The ECJ also identified that the nature of the scheme was irrelevant. Occupational pension schemes would still come within the scope of [Art 157 TFEU] whether they were employer schemes which supplemented the State's retirement scheme (as in *Bilka-Kaufhaus* (1986)) or the so-called 'contracted out schemes', which acted in place of the State scheme, as was the case here.

Key Judgment

The Court stated: 'Although it is true that many advantages granted by an employer also reflect considerations of social policy, the fact that a benefit is in the nature of pay cannot be called into question where the worker is entitled to receive the benefit in question from the employer by reason of the existence of the employment relationship.'

Key Comment

Because of the potential effects on contracted out schemes the Court decided that its ruling would not be applied retrospectively. The case, in any case, led to a flood of preliminary rulings, mainly from the UK and the Netherlands, on the precise scope of [Art 157 TFEU] in the context of occupational pension schemes.

12.2.1.5   *Handels-og Kontorfunktionaerenes Forbund v Dansk Arbejdsgiverforening for Danfoss* 109/88 [1991] ECR 3199

Key Facts

The Danish Employees' Union challenged criteria set by the Danish Employers Association as they had been applied by an employer, Danfoss. The criteria for establishing pay rates included both flexibility and seniority but, while the minimum pay for each grade was the same for both men and women, nevertheless the average pay for women within each grade was lower than for that of men.

Key Law

The ECJ held that, even though neutral criteria for setting pay might appear to be non-discriminatory, if such criteria could be shown to result in systematic discrimination this could only be because the employer applied the criteria in a discriminatory manner.

12.3.3   *Jenkins v Kingsgate Clothing Ltd* 96/80 [1981] ECR 911

Key Facts

Part-time workers in the garment industry, who were predominantly female with only one male part-time worker, were paid at a rate 10% below that of full-time workers. They challenged this as being discriminatory and contrary to [Art 157 TFEU] and Directive 75/117 (replaced by Directive 2006/54, the Recast Directive).

Key Law

In the reference, on the question of whether differences in pay rates between full-time workers and part-time workers could be discriminatory where the part-time workforce in a particular employment was predominantly female, the ECJ identified that there would be no breach of EC (now EU) law provided that the differences in pay were objectively justified and were not related to discrimination based on sex. The Court added, however, that such differences in pay could be in breach where, taking into account the difficulties that might be experienced by women in arranging to work full-time hours, the policy on pay could not be explained by factors other than discrimination on grounds of sex.

Key Comment

The Court also recognised that the mere fact that the group which is allegedly discriminated against on pay includes both men and women does not prevent there from being discrimination, otherwise a token male could always be used to defeat the women's claim. The Court also recognised the possibility of using economic arguments to justify apparent discrimination, for example where it would be uneconomic to use part-timers for the specific work.

12.3.6 *Rummler v Dato-Druck GmbH 237/85 [1986] ECR 210*

Key Facts

A female packer who had been graded by her employer under a job evaluation scheme at a point below that which she thought her work merited challenged the criteria used in the job evaluation scheme. These included the muscular effort, physical hardship and fatigue associated with the individual job.

Key Law

The ECJ held that the criteria used in job evaluation schemes must not differ according to whether the job is carried out by a man or by a woman. It also stated that it must not be organised in such a manner that it has the practical effect of discriminating against one sex. The criteria must be objectively justified and to be so they must be appropriate to the tasks to be undertaken and also correspond to a genuine need of the business. Nevertheless, the Court also stressed that it would be possible to have criteria which included factors which favoured one sex over another provided that these criteria were part of an overall package which included factors that did not. In the scheme in question other criteria which were non-discriminatory included knowledge, training and responsibility.

12.3.6 *Cadman* C-17/05) [2006]

Key Facts

Mrs Cadman worked for the Health & Safety Executive (HSE) from 1990, and by 2001 was head of a unit with an annual salary of £35,000. She complained that four male colleagues, in the same pay band, earned between £39,000 and £44,000. All had longer service, which the HSE used to justify the situation. She argued a breach of Art 157. The ECJ decided that the pay differentials could be justifiable.

Key Law

The ECJ held that different lengths of experience might justify differential pay rates for otherwise similar jobs, although this was not conclusive. It would not be so 'where the worker provides evidence capable of giving rise to serious doubts as to whether . . . the criterion of length of service is, in the circumstances, appropriate'.

Key Judgment

The Court stated that 'rewarding . . . experience acquired which enables the worker to perform his duties better constitutes a legitimate objective of pay policy. As a general rule . . . the criterion of length of service is appropriate to attain that objective. Length of service goes hand in hand with experience, and experience generally enables the worker to perform his duties better'.

Key Comment

What the case does demonstrate is that incremental pay scales can be justified on the basis of length of experience leading to better ability to do the job, but that an excessive amount of increment is unjustified and potentially discriminatory.

Key Problem

Although the Court focused on objective justification for particular criteria within an overall package that did not discriminate, in accepting physical strength as an acceptable criteria it does seem to be allowing employers to set criteria that would naturally discriminate against women and in favour of men.

12.3.6

Murphy v An Bord Telecom Eireann 157/86 [1988] ECR 673

Key Facts

A female skilled factory worker discovered that she and 28 colleagues were being paid less than a male employee, an unskilled store labourer. She challenged this in the national courts and, following a job evaluation study, was informed that her work was actually of greater value than that of her male comparator and, since the work was of unequal value no equal pay claim was possible. The case was referred to the ECJ.

Key Law

The ECJ held that despite the fact that [Art 157 TFEU] and Directive 75/117 (replaced by Directive 2006/54, the Recast Directive) referred to the principle of equal pay for work of equal value, this could not be used as a ground for justifying the discrimination or for dismissing her claim to equal pay in the circumstances.

Key Judgment

The Court stated that 'to adopt a contrary interpretation would be tantamount to rendering the principle of equal pay ineffective . . . an employer would easily be able to circumvent the principle by assigning additional or more onerous duties to workers of a particular sex, who could then be paid a lower wage'.

12.4.4   *Johnston v Chief Constable of the Royal Ulster Constabulary* 222/84 [1987] QB 129

Key Facts

A female officer in the Royal Ulster Constabulary claimed that the policy of not issuing firearms to female officers was in breach of the right of equal treatment under Directive 76/207 [now 2006/54] and that the policy acted in effect as a bar to promotion for female officers. The RUC claimed that the policy was justified on grounds of public safety and national security and was also authorised by a statutory instrument. It also argued that to allow women to carry arms would increase their risk of becoming targets for assassination and that the derogation [then under Art 2(2) of Directive 76/207] would apply. The Secretary of State for Northern Ireland issued Mrs Johnston with a certificate confirming the point conclusively.

Key Law

The Court held that there was no general public safety exemption to the equal treatment principle in the Directive. It also stated that the only derogation available was that in Art 2 of the Directive, on occupational activities which by reason of their nature or the context in which they operate mean that the sex of the worker is a determining factor. It held that the derogation should be applied strictly but accepted that the principle of proportionality should also be applied. The policy could fall within the derogation because of the politically sensitive situation then in Northern Ireland.

Key Comment

The ECJ did recognise that the effect of the certificate was to deprive female officers of the right to a judicial hearing or indeed any remedy. As such it was a breach of human rights.

12.4.4   *Kalanke v Frei Hausestadt Bremen* C-450/93 [1995] ECR I-3051

Key Facts

A male applicant for a post complained about the appointment of a female applicant where both had equal qualifications and the justification for the appointment was a German law giving preference to female applicants where there was an under-representation of females at the level of the post in question.

Key Law

The ECJ held that the exemption to promote equal opportunity and to remove existing inequality [then contained in Art 2(4) of Directive 76/207 could not apply. This was because the purpose of the provision was to allow measures to eliminate actual instances of inequality, not to establish any absolute priority for women or positive discrimination.

Key Problem

The case caused uproar in certain quarters and there were some calls for Art 2(4) to be extended to allow for positive discrimination in order to assist in removing current levels of inequality. However, subsequent case law that has distinguished from *Kalanke* would seem to have taken care of the problem.

Key Link

Marschall v Land Nordrhein-Westfalen C-409/95 [1997] ECR I-6363 p 125.

12.4.4

Marschall v Land Nordrhein-Westfalen C-409/95 [1997] ECR I-6363

Key Facts

A male teacher, a German national, applied for a promotion in a comprehensive school in Germany but was rejected because there were fewer women than men in his particular career bracket and so a similarly qualified woman was given the post. The justification for the decision was under German law, which provided that women with equal qualifications and suitability were to be given priority in such appointments unless reasons specific to an individual male candidate tilted the balance in his favour. The man challenged this 'positive discrimination' as being unlawful under Directive 76/207 [now 2006/54].

Key Law

The ECJ distinguished *Kalanke* (1995) on the basis of this qualifying clause and held that such a clause made the measure non-discriminatory by contrast to those measures that merely confer automatic priority for women.

12.4.5

Dekker v Stichting Vormingscentrum voor Jong Volwassenen (VJV Centrum) Plus C-177/88 [1990] ECR I-3941

Key Facts

A woman was refused employment because she was pregnant. She claimed this was direct discrimination. The company to whom she had applied for employment argued that there were no male candidates for the post so there could be no discrimination when they chose from an exclusively female file of candidates.

Key Law

The ECJ rejected the company's argument and held that refusal to employ a woman because she was pregnant was directly linked to her sex and amounted to direct discrimination and was unjustifiable.

Key Judgment

The Court stated that 'A refusal of employment on account of the financial consequences of absence due to pregnancy must be regarded as based, essentially on the fact of pregnancy [and] cannot be justified on grounds relating to the financial loss which an employer who appointed a pregnant woman would suffer for the duration of her maternity leave'.

12.4.5

Webb v EMO Air Cargo C-2/93 [1992] ECR I-3567

Key Facts

A female worker was appointed by a small business with only 16 employees to cover maternity leave for one of them. When she was taken on it was envisaged that she should be able to stay with the firm even after the end of the maternity leave that she was covering. After she had been in employment for two weeks she found that she was pregnant and when her employer was informed she was promptly dismissed. She then brought a claim in a tribunal for unfair dismissal on the ground that the sole reason for her dismissal was her pregnancy and that this was therefore discriminatory.

Key Law

The Court in the reference held that dismissal of a female worker in an indefinite period of employment solely for reasons of her pregnancy did amount to unlawful discrimination contrary to Directive 76/207 [now 2006/54]. The question left open by the Court was whether the dismissal would be non-discriminatory and therefore lawful if the employment was for a definite period.

Key Link

Jiménez Melgar v Ayuntamiento de Los Barrios C-438/99 [2001] ECR I-6915 and *Teledenmark v Handels-og Kontorfuntionaererernes Forbund i Danmark* C-109/00 [2001] ECR I-6993. In both cases the ECJ held that no distinction should be drawn between pregnant workers on indefinite contracts and those on temporary contracts.

12.4.6   ### *Burton v British Railways Board* 19/81 [1982] ECR 555

Key Facts

A railway worker wishing to retire at age 58 challenged his employer's voluntary redundancy scheme, which was eligible to women at age 55 and men not until 60. Since this fell within an exemption in the Sex Discrimination Act 1975 his only possible claim was under Directive 76/207 [now 2006/54].

Key Law

The ECJ held that the Directive applied in principle to access to voluntary redundancy schemes. However, as the ages for voluntary redundancy were calculated according to different statutory retirement ages for men and women, which was permitted under Directive 79/7, then the claim under Directive 76/207 would fail.

Prais v The Council 130/75 [1976] ECR 1589

Key Facts

A Jewish woman applied for a post as a Community (now EU) official, not mentioning her faith in the application.

When she had to sit an exam in support of her application on a specific date she then explained that this was impossible as it fell on an important Jewish festival. She was then prevented from completing the exam because the Council decided that it was necessary for all candidates to sit the exam on the same day. She challenged this decision.

Key Law

The Court recognised that freedom of religion was an essential principle of [EU] Law and that people should not be disadvantaged because of their religion. However, the Court upheld the decision of Council since it had not been informed in advance of the difficulty, which therefore prevented it from making the necessary arrangements to avoid the discrimination on religion.

P v S C-13/94 [1996] ECR I-2143

Key Facts

A male employee of a Cornwall college informed his Director of Studies that he was to undergo 'gender reassignment' to become a woman, which would involve a period of dressing and behaving like a woman and would ultimately result in surgery for a full sex change. He was later dismissed and claimed that this was unlawful sexual discrimination and therefore a breach of Directive 76/207.

Key Law

The question for the ECJ was whether dismissal of a transsexual was not for reasons of gender since it did not involve in effect a single gender. The Court held that the Directive could not be viewed in such a narrow way. The whole purpose of the Directive was to prevent discrimination and promote equality, which was, in any case, a fundamental principle of law to be applied universally. It rejected the view submitted by the British Government that the dismissal was not discriminatory since it could have equally applied to a female to male transsexual. The transsexual was being discriminated against by being treated less favourably than a person of the sex to which he/she had belonged prior to the gender reassignment.

Grant v South West Trains Ltd C-249/96 [1998] ECR I-621

Key Facts

An employer provided concessionary rail travel for its employees in respect of legal spouses and cohabitees of the opposite sex. Grant tried to claim concessionary travel on behalf of her lesbian partner and was rejected. She claimed that this was discriminatory.

Key Law

The ECJ appeared to narrow to an extent the broad principle stated in *P v S*, although with sound reason. The Court held that the policy could not be discriminatory since it did not treat female workers differently, and therefore less favourably, than male workers. The provision in the contract would apply in the same way to male homosexuals so the discrimination was not based on sex.

Key Comment

This position changed with the introduction of Art 13 in the Treaty of Amsterdam and the Framework Directive which gave the Council the power to take action to remove discrimination based on sex, race or ethnic origin, religion and belief, disability, age and sexual orientation.

KB v National Health Service Pensions Agency C-117/01 [2004] All ER (EC) 1089

Key Facts

Transsexuals could not marry under English law. The National Health Service Pension Scheme provided benefits for widows and widowers of members of the scheme but there was no provision for unmarried partners. This rule was challenged as discriminatory.

Key Law

The ECJ held that the rules combined in this way constituted a breach of EC (now EU) law and based its reasoning on recent cases in the European Court of Human Rights identifying that the rule preventing transsexuals from marrying breached Art 12 of the Convention.

13 The social dimension

▶ 13.1 Art 20 and citizenship

1 TEU laid the foundations of citizenship – a logical progression of the move away from the purely economic view of free movement – now in Art 20.

2 Arts 21–25 state the individual rights of citizens:

- to move and reside freely in Member States – Art 21; subject to Member States' rules on nationality (*R v Secretary of State for the Home Department, ex parte Kaur* C-192/99); while it is questionable whether Art 21 is directly effective (*Grzelczyk v Centre Public d'Aide Sociale* C-184/99) it is possible to rely on it in national proceedings (*Zhu and Chen v Secretary of State for the Home Department* C-200/02); and it has been used in respect of migrant students' right to a maintenance loan (*Bidar* C-209/03) or grant (*Morgan v Bezirksregierung Koin and Iris Butcher v Landrat des Breises Duren* C-11/06 and C-12/06), and social security benefits (*Collins* C-138/02 *and Ioannidis* C-258/04), and the compatibility of national legislation on tax (*Schempp* C-403/03) and employment (*De Cuyper* C-406/04) on Art 21 rights;

- to vote and stand as a candidate in municipal elections – Art 21(1);

- to vote in or stand for the European Parliament – Art 21(2);

- to receive diplomatic protection or representation in a state where the citizen's own state is not diplomatically represented – Art 23;

- to petition the European Parliament or apply to the ombudsman – Art 24.

3 Those derogations found in the Treaty can be applied.

4 However, complete free movement will only be achieved with removal of all border controls – all Member States other than the UK and Eire accepted this principle in the Schengen Agreement.

5 The Amsterdam Treaty integrated policy on free movement, asylum, and immigration – a five-year period was set for implementation, e.g. of

removal of all internal border controls. The ToL provided for the integration of the Schengen Agreement into the framework of the EU and includes all Member States except the UK and Eire.

6   Problems concerning concept of citizenship include:

● it is symbolic, without real content;

● the rights and duties involved are not totally clear;

● it adds little to citizenship of individual states;

● non-citizens enjoy similar rights in many cases;

● it misleadingly suggests the concept of a European state which does not yet exist.

7   But the general idea is to promote a sense of connection with the Union as a whole, as well as with Member States.

▶ 13.2 Social policy

13.2.1 Background

1   There was no direct mention of social policy in the EC Treaty – policies were originally framed in economic terms.

2   But Arts 136–145 (now Arts 151–161 TFEU) did set out general aims of 'improved working conditions and standard of living' and Art 130d established the European Social Fund (ESF).

3   It is said that the social dimension has consistently been compromised by the overriding economic interest.

4   There was little progress in social policy before the mid-1980s, though the first 'Social Action Programme' (1974) did set out objectives of full and better employment; better living and working conditions; social dialogue in the workplace.

5   With change of personnel, e.g. Mitterand, Delors, a new 'Social Action Programme' was agreed, stressing the need for a 'balanced Europe' and 'social and economic cohesion'.

6   Art 118a and Art 118b were inserted in the Treaty by SEA '86.

7   Followed by 'The Social Dimension of the Internal Market', recommending creation of a Social Charter, accepted by all but rejected out of hand by the UK – resulted in the Social Protocol following Maastricht.

8   ToA was the most important development for social policy, and introduced a new framework, after the UK agreed.

13.2.2 The Social Charter

1   This is implemented through Social Action Programmes.

2   It lays down 13 fundamental principles to achieve:

- ● right of free movement for employment;
- ● right to fair remuneration;
- ● right to employment on same terms as nationals;
- ● right to improved living and working conditions;
- ● right to social protection in existing national systems, and minimum income for those without employment;
- ● right to free association and collective bargaining;
- ● right to vocational training;
- ● right of men and women to equal treatment in and out of work;
- ● rights of workers to information, consultation, and to participation;
- ● right to protection of health and safety at work;
- ● protection of children and adolescents;
- ● guaranteed minimum standard of living for the elderly;
- ● improvements in both social and professional integration for the disabled.

13.2.3 Treaty of Amsterdam and the new framework

1   A new Art 136 (now Art 151 TFEU) was inserted, which recognises the Charter and states new objectives: 'promotion of employment, improved living and working conditions, . . . proper social protection, dialogue between management and labour, development of human resources with a view to lasting high employment and combating of exclusion . . .'.

2   But it is limited by subsidiarity and economic realism.

3   Art 137 (now Art 152 TFEU), using Qualified Majority Voting, was the method chosen to implement objectives including: improvement of working environment; information and consultation of workers; integration of those excluded from the labour market; equality between men and women.

13.2.4 The European Social Fund

1   The purpose of the fund in Art 162 is to improve employment opportunities for workers and contribute, thereby, to raising the standard of living.

2   It is administered by the Commission.

3   It was originally used very much to combat youth unemployment, but the overriding principle now is to complement forms of aid already emanating from national programmes rather than creating entirely new programmes of aid.

4   Education is, in any case, helped mainly through funding systems such as ERASMUS.

▶ 13.3 Protection of workers

1   Apart from free movement and equality there are a number of ways that EU law has sought to protect workers.

2   Commonly these are introduced as Directives through the area of health and safety – Art 151 refers to the promotion and maintenance of improved working conditions.

3   Although the definition of working conditions is deliberately vague, Arts 153–156 refer specifically to employment rights, health and safety, training, social security.

4   General standards have been introduced in legislation including: safety and health of workers at work (Directive 89/391); safety and health of pregnant workers (Directive 92/85); protection of young workers (Directive 94/33); parental leave (Directive 96/34); protection for part-time workers (Directive 97/81); protection for fixed-term workers (Directive 1999/70).

5   Directive 2003/88 (replacing 93/104) (the Working Time Directive) – is a contentious piece of legislation introduced under the old Art 118a – now found in Art 153.

    ● The Directive lays down minimum standards in organising working time, and so maximum work periods (48 hours per week) and minimum rest periods (11 hours out of 24, and 48 hours in every seven-day period) – different periods apply to young workers.

    ● It also lays down standards in relation to things such as night work.

- It also provides for minimum paid holidays – four weeks.
- But it also allows for wide derogations.

6   Directive 2001/23, consolidating Directive 98/50 (the Acquired Rights Directive), protects workers when the business they work for is transferred.

- Incorporated in the UK as Transfer of Undertakings (Protection of Employment) Regulations (TUPE).
- It basically transfers rights and obligations to the new employer when there is a 'relevant transfer'.
- The Directive modified and amended Directive 77/187.

7   Directive 98/59 (the Collective Redundancies Directive) applies to those situations where, for example, the whole workforce may be made redundant:

- it provides for proper consultation procedures;
- and attempts to avoid the redundancy if possible.

8   Directive 80/987 provides state protection for employees of insolvent employers.

▶ 13.4 Protection of consumers

1   Before SEA there was little reference in Treaties to consumer protection.

2   Those measures that were introduced had as much to do with protecting free competition as anything else.

3   Prior to this time, measures were introduced under the old Art 100 (now Art 115) aiming for harmonisation, including:

- the Product Liability Directive 85/374:
  - i)   this imposed strict liability on producers for all damage caused by defective products;
  - ii) 'producer' was defined broadly so as to include anyone in the chain of supply and distribution, including importers;
- the Misleading Advertising Directive 84/450;
- the Doorstep Selling Directive 85/577;
- the Consumer Credit Directive 87/102.

4   SEA, to speed up harmonisation, took to adopting measures under Art 100a, allowing qualified majority voting.

5   Measures introduced by the old Art 100a (now Art 114) were included:

- the Toy Safety Directive 88/378;

- the Price Indication Directive 88/314;

- the Package Travel Directive 90/314;

- the Unfair Terms in Consumer Contracts Directive 93/13.

6   Following Maastricht and the TEU, consumer protection was accepted as a policy of the EU:

- to be achieved by internal market measures under Art 114, and specific actions using the co-decision procedure;

- measures subsequently adopted include the Timeshare Directive 94/47, and the Cross-Border Transfer Directive 97/5.

7   The Treaty of Amsterdam also made a commitment to consumer protection in Art 153 (now Art 169 TFEU), which will be by adopting measures under Art 114, or by adopting measures that support the policies of Member States which include the Distance Selling Directive 97/7, the Timeshare Directive 94/47, the Cross-Border Transfer Directive 97/5 and the Electronic Commerce Directive 2000/31.

▶ 13.5 The Charter of Rights

1   Protection of human rights is a general principle of EU law that judges in the ECJ use in interpretation.

2   However, despite many examples of the ECJ referring to the European Convention of Human Rights, and while all Member States are signatories to the European Convention, there is no formal link between the EU and the Convention.

3   The EU has developed its own 'Charter of Fundamental Rights', the first draft being produced in July 2000.

4   It was formally considered by heads of state at the Biarritz summit in October 2000, and formally adopted by the European Council at the Nice summit in December 2000.

5   The rights identified in the Charter very much overlap with Convention rights – the right to life, the right to personal liberty, protection of workers' rights, protection from discrimination, protection of personal data, etc.

6   The preamble to the Charter states that it is intended to 'enhance protection of human rights in light of changes in society, social progress, and scientific and technical developments'.

7   The Charter was given legal force in Art 16(1) TEU as amended by ToL:

- however, it does not create fundamental rights that are of general application in national law;

- neither does it extend the application of EU law;

- UK and Poland were concerned that there was no indirect incorporation of the Charter into their own law – so there are no justiciable rights in UK and Poland arising from the Charter except those where the two states have already provided for them in national law.

Key Cases Checklist

Micheletti v Delegacion del Gobierno en Cantabria C-369/90 [1992] ECR I-4239

Key Facts

An individual born in Argentina to Italian parents and with dual nationality wished to set up as a dentist in Spain. Spanish authorities rejected his application as Spanish law deemed him to have the nationality of his country of birth.

Key Law

The ECJ held that, as he had dual nationality, he was an EU citizen and could invoke rights under [Art 49 TFEU].

13.1.2   ### *Collins v Secretary of State for Work and Pensions* C-138/02 [2004] 3 WLR 1236

Key Facts

An individual with dual American and Irish nationality applied for jobseeker's allowance in the UK but was refused because he was not 'habitually resident' in the UK as required by enabling regulations. EU workers under Regulation 1612/68 and those with rights of residence under Directive 68/360 (now in Directive 2004/38) were exempt from the rule.

Key Law

The ECJ held that, although a job seeker under Antonissen (1991), he was protected against discrimination on nationality by [Art 18 TFEU] as he was a citizen by virtue of [Art 20 TFEU]. The 'habitual residence' requirement was discriminatory, although it was objectively justifiable.

13.1.2

R v Secretary of State for the Home Department, ex p Kaur C-192/99 [2001] All ER (EC) 250

Key Facts

A Kenyan Asian gained UK citizenship under the British Nationality Act 1948 but did not fall under any category under the Immigration Act 1971 entitling UK residence. The British Nationality Act 1981 then gave her British Overseas Citizen status but again no right of residence. When she entered the UK she applied for right to remain and take up employment but was rejected by the Home Secretary. She sought judicial review on the basis of [Art 20 TFEU] and [Art 21 TFEU].

Key Law

The ECJ held that she could not have EU citizenship purely on the basis of her British Overseas Citizen status since this would give her the right to travel freely through the EU and reside anywhere but the UK.

Key Comment

To give her EU citizenship would clearly have been illogical in the circumstances. It is plain that a person can invoke Art 21 TFEU only if they already have a right of residence in at least one Member State.

13.1.2

Grzelczyk v Centre Public d'Aide Sociale C-184/99 [2003] All ER (EC) 385

Key Facts

A French national studying in Belgium sought financial assistance so he could concentrate on his studies rather than support himself by part-time work. He was refused because of his nationality and challenged this on the basis of [Art 21 TFEU], the right of free movement.

Key Law

The ECJ held that he had been discriminated against directly under [Art 18 TFEU] so the only question was whether he fell within the terms for granting the assistance. As a migrant student he should receive the same benefits as students from the host state, so was entitled.

Baumbast v Secretary of State for the Home Department C-413/99 [2002] ECR I-7091

Key Facts

A German national, his Colombian wife, his eldest daughter from a previous relationship, with dual German and Colombian nationality, and their youngest daughter, with only Colombian nationality, lived in the UK for three years with the German working or self-employed during that time. He then took work in China and then in Lesotho. His wife applied for indefinite leave to reside in the UK for herself and her daughters but was refused as she was not an EU citizen and her husband could no longer be classed as a worker as he worked outside of the EU.

Key Law

The ECJ held that [Art 21 TFEU] was directly effective and could be relied on by citizens. The wife had rights of residence as primary carer of the eldest daughter, an EU citizen by virtue of her dual nationality.

Key Comment

The ECJ also identified that, though [Art 21 TFEU] was subject to limitations, Member States should only apply these limitations subject to other principles such as proportionality.

D'Hoop v Office National de l'Emploi C-224/98 [2003] All ER (EC) 527

Key Facts

A Belgian national undertook secondary education in Belgium and then undergraduate study in France. After graduating she applied for a benefit normally paid to graduates of Belgian universities who had also completed school education in Belgium and was refused because of her schooling in France.

Key Law

The ECJ held that the rule was discrimination on nationality contrary to [Art 18 TFEU] and that she could rely on her citizenship rights under [Art 21 TFEU] and receive the allowance.

13.1.2 *Zhu and Chen v Secretary of State for the Home Department* C-200/02 [2004] 3 WLR 1453

Key Facts

A Chinese couple with one child wished to avoid a Chinese law allowing only one child and to have another so, while six months pregnant, the woman moved to the UK and gave birth. Although the child was born in Northern Ireland, under Irish law any person born in any part of Ireland gained Irish nationality. She then moved to Wales and their right to residence was challenged by authorities.

Key Law

The ECJ held that the child, having Irish nationality, was an EU citizen, so the mother was entitled to residence of unlimited duration as the child's primary carer.

Key Judgment

The Court identified that 'A refusal to allow the parent, whether a national of a Member State or ... of a non-member country, who is the carer of a child ... to reside with that child in the host Member State would deprive the child's right of residence of any useful effect ... accordingly the carer must be [allowed] to reside with the child in the host Member State for the duration of the residence'.

Key Link

Carpenter v Secretary of State for the Home Department C-60/00 [2003] QB 416, where the same principle was applied to the Filipino wife of a UK national providing services in other Member States as she cared for his children from his first marriage, so to deport her would prevent him from running his business in breach of Art 49 (now Art 56 TFEU).

Hertz v Aldi Marked 179/88 [1990] ECR I-3979

Key Facts

A part-time cashier was dismissed when she was repeatedly absent from work because of illness which, although connected to pregnancy and childbirth, actually occurred some time afterwards.

Key Law

The ECJ held that, although under Art 10 of the Safety and Health at Work of Pregnant Workers Directive 92/85, a dismissal during pregnancy or maternity leave is prohibited, here it was impossible to say that the dismissal discriminated against her on grounds of her sex. This was because it was also impossible to distinguish between her illness at that time and any illness suffered by a man who might be subject to the same dismissal procedure.

Key Comment

It was obviously also crucial to the decision that the illness occurred between a year and two years after her maternity leave expired.

Wippel C-313/02 [2005] 1 CMLR 9

Key Facts

An Austrian employee was contracted on a 'work on demand' basis with no fixed hours or income. She was also able to refuse the work. Eventually she brought an action seeking to class herself as a part-time worker for the protections that this offered.

Key Law

The ECJ held that it was for Member States to determine whether a particular worker was a part-timer and therefore within the scope of the Protection for Part-Time Workers Directive 97/81.

Key Problem

Under clause 2(2) of the Directive, Member States may exclude part-time workers who are classed as casual. This has the effect of denying those workers the right to enforce clause 4(1), which requires that part-time workers should not be treated less favourably than full-time workers merely because they work part-time unless this can be objectively justified.

SIMAP C-303/89 [2000] ECR I-7963

Key Facts

During litigation between a Spanish doctors' union and the Health Ministry, the question arose whether time spent at home 'on call' counted towards working time for the purposes of determining the maximum weekly working time under Art 6 of the Working Time [Directive 2003/88].

Key Law

The ECJ held that while being 'on call' at the hospital did count towards the working week, being on call at home did not.

Key Judgment

As the Court said, this was because 'in that situation doctors may manage their time with fewer constraints and pursue their own interests'.

Jaeger C-151/02 [2003] ECR I-8389

Key Facts

A German doctor was required to spend part of his week 'on call'. This had to be spent at the hospital and he was required to attend a patient only when the need arose. When he was not needed he could sleep in a bedroom at the hospital. He argued that this 'on call' period should count towards his average weekly working hours, while his employer maintained that the time he spent in bed was his rest period.

Key Law

The ECJ applied SIMAP (2000), and held that, for the purposes of Art 3 of the Working Time Directive [Directive 2003/88], the entire period on call should count towards his working week.

Key Judgment

The Court identified that 'The objective of [the Directive] is to secure the effective protection of the safety and health of employees by allowing them to enjoy minimum periods of rest'. It also acknowledged that in the case of junior doctors 'the periods during which their services are not required ... may ... be of short duration and/or subject to frequent interruption' and that they 'may be prompted to intervene ... to monitor the condition of patients'.

Key Link

Pfeiffer & Others C-397–403/01 [2005] 1 CMLR 44, where periods of inactivity of German Red Cross workers 'on call' during emergencies were not counted as working time in German legislation, which the ECJ held had incorrectly implemented the Working Time Directive.

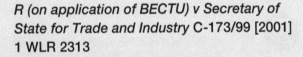

R (on application of BECTU) v Secretary of State for Trade and Industry C-173/99 [2001] 1 WLR 2313

Key Facts

The Broadcasting, Entertainment, Cinematographic and Theatre Union (BECTU) alleged that its members were being unfairly denied paid annual leave contrary to [the Working Time Directive 2003/88]. Its argument was based on the fact that the majority of members were employed under short-term contracts and under Regulation 13 of Working Time Regulations 1988 (which had implemented the Directive) annual leave entitlement only applied to employees of more than 13 weeks' continuous service.

Key Law

The ECJ, in one of the first references on the Directive, held that the UK had failed to properly implement the Directive by imposing conditional requirements for entitlement when there was nothing in the Directive permitting such a provision.

Gibson v East Riding of Yorkshire Council [1999] IRLR 359

Key Facts

A swimming instructor employed by a school was not required to work during the school holidays and received no wages for that time under her contract. She brought an action in an Employment Tribunal claiming that she was in effect being denied her right under Art 7 of the Working Time Directive to paid annual leave. The Tribunal held that her employer, the local council, was an emanation of the state for the purposes of vertical direct effect but that the provision was conditional and therefore failed the *Van Gend en Loos* (1963) criteria for direct effect.

Key Law

The Employment Appeal Tribunal reversed this decision and held that the Directive was directly effective vertically so that the woman was entitled to paid leave.

Richards C-423/04 [2006] ECR I-3585

Key Facts

Sarah Richards was born, as a man, in February 1942, later diagnosed with gender dysphoria, and underwent gender reassignment surgery in May 2001. In February 2002 she applied for a retirement pension having reached 60, the pension age for women at that time. This was rejected, she appealed, and the case was referred to the ECJ.

Key Law

It was held that she had suffered discrimination on grounds of sex in breach of Art 4(1) of Directive 79/7.

Key Judgment

The ECJ explained that 'The scope of Directive 79/7 cannot thus be confined simply to discrimination based on the fact that a person is of one or other sex. In view of its purpose and the nature of the rights which it seeks to safeguard, the scope of that directive is also such as to apply to discrimination arising from the gender reassignment of the person concerned'.

Wolf C-229/08 [2010] ECR I-1

Key Facts

Wolf, who was aged 31, applied for a job as a fireman in Frankfurt. His application was rejected because under German law, the maximum age for recruitment was 30. Wolf argued that the German legislation constituted direct discrimination on grounds of age, in breach of the Framework Directive.

Key Law

The Court held that the maximum age limit for firemen was permitted by Art 4(1), as to 'ensure the operational capacity and proper functioning of the professional fire service' was a legitimate aim. The 'possession of especially high physical capacities' could be regarded as a 'genuine and determining occupational requirement'. The need for full physical capacity to carry on that activity was related to age, since (according to scientific data submitted by the German Government) few over 45 have sufficient physical capacity to perform fire-fighting activities.

Appendix

Table of equivalent numbering in EC Treaty, after ToA, and after ToL in TFEU

ECTreaty	After ToA	After ToL in TFEU
Art 2	Art 2 (repealed)	Art 3 (TEU)
–	–	Art 3 (new)
Art 3a	Art 4	Art 4
Art 3b	Art 5	Art 5
Art 3g	Art 6	Art 11
–	–	Art 6 (new)
Art 4	Art 7 (repealed)	–
Art 5	Art 10	Art 4 (TEU)
–	–	Art 7 (new)
Art 6	Art 12	Art 18
Art 8	Art 17	Art 20
–	Art 16 (new)	Art 14
Art 8a	Art 18	Art 21
Art 8c	Art 20	Art 23
Art 8d	Art 21	Art 24
Art 7	Art 14	Art 26
Art 9	Art 23	Art 28
Art 10	Art 24	Art 29
Art 12	Art 25	Art 30

Art 13	Art 26	Art 31
Art 28	Art 41	Art 47
Art 29	Art 27	Art 32
Art 30	Art 28	Art 34
Art 34	Art 29	Art 35
Art 36	Art 30	Art 36
Art 42	Art 36	Art 42
Art 48	Art 39	Art 45
Art 49	Art 40	Art 46
Art 51	Art 42	Art 48
Art 52	Art 43	Art 49
Art 54	Art 44	Art 50
Art 55	Art 45	Art 51
Art 56	Art 46	Art 52
Art 57	Art 47	Art 53
Art 58	Art 48	Art 54
Art 59	Art 49	Art 56
Art 60	Art 50	Art 57
Art 61	Art 51	Art 58
Art 63	Art 52	Art 59
Art 64	Art 53	Art 60
Art 65	Art 54	Art 61
Art 66	Art 55	Art 62
Art 73c	Art 57	Art 64
Art 73i	Art 61	Art 67
–	–	Art 68 (new)
–	–	Art 69 (new)
–	–	Art 70 (new)

–	Art 36 (TEU)	Art 71
Art 73l	Art 64(1) (part)	Art 72
	Art 33 (TEU)	
–	–	Art 73 (new)
Art 73n	Art 66	Art 74
Art 73g	Art 60	Art 75
–	–	Art 76 (new)
Art 73j	Art 62	Art 77
Art 73k	Art 63 (part)	Art 78
Art 73l	Art 64 (part)	
Art 73k	Art 63 (part)	Art 79
–	–	Art 80 (new)
Art 73m	Art 65	Art 81
–	Art 31 (TEU)	Art 82
–	Art 31 (TEU)	Art 83
–	–	Art 84 (new)
–	Art 31 (TEU)	Art 85
–	–	Art 86 (new)
–	Art 30 (TEU)	Art 87
–	Art 30 (TEU)	Art 88
–	Art 32 (TEU)	Art 89
Art 85	Art 81	Art 101
Art 86	Art 82	Art 102
Art 90	Art 86	Art 106
Art 95	Art 90	Art 110
Art 100	Art 94	Art 115
Art 100a	Art 95	Art 114
Art 113	Art 133	Art 207

Art 117	Art 136	Art 151
–	–	Art 152 (new)
Art 118	Art 137	Art 153
Art 118a	Art 138	Art 154
Art 118b	Art 139	Art 155
Art 118c	Art 140	Art 156
Art 119	Art 141	Art 157
Art 119a	Art 142	Art 158
Art 120	Art 143	Art 159
Art 121	Art 144	Art 160
Art 122	Art 145	Art 161
Art 123	Art 146	Art 162
Art 129a	Art 153	Art 169
Art 130d	Art 150	Art 166
Art 138	Art 190 (part)	Art 223
Art 138a	Art 191 (part)	Art 224
Art 138b	Art 192 (part)	Art 225
Art 138c	Art 193	Art 226
Art 138d	Art 194	Art 227
Art 138e	Art 195	Art 228
Art 139	Art 196	Art 229
Art 140	Art 197 (part)	Art 230
Art 141	Art 198	Art 231
Art 142	Art 199	Art 232
Art 143	Art 200	Art 233
Art 144	Art 201	Art 234
Art 145	Art 202	Art 16 (TEU)
Art 147	Art 204	Art 237

Art 148	Art 205	Art 16 (TEU)
Art 148	Art 205 (part)	Art 238
Art 150	Art 206	Art 239
Art 151	Art 207	Art 240
Art 152	Art 208	Art 241
Art 153	Art 209	Art 242
Art 154	Art 210	Art 243
–	–	Art 244 (new)
Art 157	Art 213	Art 245
Art 164	Art 220	Art 19 (TEU)
Art 159	Art 215	Art 246
Art 160	Art 216	Art 247
Art 161	Art 217 (part)	Art 248
Art 162	Art 218 (part)	Art 249
Art 163	Art 219	Art 250
Art 165	Art 221 (part)	Art 251
Art 166	Art 222	Art 252
Art 167	Art 223	Art 253
Art 168	Art 224	Art 254
–	–	Art 255 (new)
Art 168a	Art 225	Art 256
Art 168a	Art 225a	Art 257
Art 169	Art 226	Art 258
Art 170	Art 227	Art 259
Art 171	Art 228	Art 260
Art 172	Art 229	Art 261
Art 172	Art 229a	Art 262
Art 173	Art 230	Art 263

Art 174	Art 231	Art 264
Art 175	Art 232	Art 265
Art 176	Art 233	Art 266
Art 177	Art 234	Art 267
Art 178	Art 235	Art 268
–	–	Art 269 (new)
Art 178	Art 236	Art 270
Art 180	Art 237	Art 271
Art 181	Art 238	Art 272
Art 182	Art 239	Art 273
Art 183	Art 240	Art 274
–	–	Art 275 (new)
–	–	Art 276 (new)
Art 184	Art 241	Art 277
Art 185	Art 242	Art 278
Art 186	Art 243	Art 279
Art 187	Art 244	Art 280
Art 188	Art 245	Art 281
Art 189	Art 249	Art 288
–	–	Art 289 (new)
Art 198d	Art 266	Art 308
Art 215	Art 288	Art 340
Art 229	Art 302	Art 220
Art 230	Art 303	
Art 231	Art 304	
Art 235	Art 308	Art 352
Art 238	Art 310	Art 354

Index

In this index Treaties are entered under the first word following Treaty; e.g,
Lisbon, Treaty of (ToL)